THE WAY OF THE CHAMPION

THE WAY OF THE CHAMPION

Pain,
Persistence,
and the
Path Forward

PAUL RABIL

PORTFOLIO / PENGUIN

Portfolio / Penguin
An imprint of Penguin Random House LLC
penguinrandomhouse.com

Most Portfolio books are available at a discount when purchased in
quantity for sales promotions or corporate use. Special editions,
which include personalized covers, excerpts, and corporate
imprints, can be created when purchased in large quantities.
For more information, please call (212) 572-2232 or email
specialmarkets@penguinrandomhouse.com. Your local bookstore
can also assist with discounted bulk purchases using the
Penguin Random House corporate Business-to-Business
program. For assistance in locating a participating retailer,
email B2B@penguinrandomhouse.com.

Library of Congress Cataloging-in-Publication Data

Names: Rabil, Paul, author.
Title: The way of the champion: pain, persistence, and the path
  forward / Paul Rabil.
Description: New York: Portfolio/Penguin, [2024]
Identifiers: LCCN 2023056715 (print) |
  LCCN 2023056716 (ebook) | ISBN 9780593545492 (hardcover) |
  ISBN 9780593545508 (ebook)
Subjects: LCSH: Rabil, Paul. | Success. | Conduct of life. |
  Lacrosse players—United States.
Classification: LCC BJ1611.2 .R33 2024 (print) |
  LCC BJ1611.2 (ebook) | DDC 650.1—dc23/eng/20240117
LC record available at https://lccn.loc.gov/2023056715
LC ebook record available at https://lccn.loc.gov/2023056716

Printed in the United States of America
1st Printing

BOOK DESIGN BY NICOLE LAROCHE

To the hopeful, the determined, and the dreamers.
May this book serve as a source of guidance as you
navigate the challenges and successes that await you.

Remember, your journey will be a tribute to
the legacy of those who came before us.

A champion must forget greatness and must be simply the man that you have to beat at his best under pressure.

—BILL RUSSELL

CONTENTS

BOOK 1 AMATEUR

BOOK 2 PROFESSIONAL

BOOK 3 BEYOND THE GAME

In the realm of sports, there exists a unique and unwavering pursuit of excellence—a relentless journey taken by those who strive not just for victory, but for mastery. This path is marked by commitment, preparation, and sacrifice. Of course, there are challenges and setbacks that test one's resolve. This path will transcend winning and losing—reaching into the very core of what it means to compete. Amid the chaos and uncertainty, a champion emerges.

Throughout my years in the world of professional football, I have had the privilege to witness firsthand the embodiment of this way of the champion in the athletes and teams that have left an indelible mark on the sport. The road to championships is not merely paved with physical prowess; it requires mental fortitude, strategic acumen, and an unshakable belief in one's ability to overcome any obstacle.

The first time I met Paul Rabil was during his junior year in college at Johns Hopkins University. I was visiting their lacrosse practice to observe when he asked his head coach, Dave Pietramala, if he could get ten minutes with me when they finished. It was in that office after practice that Paul must have asked me thirty questions in under ten minutes. He wanted to know what it takes to be a champion, how the best leaders show up for their team, and he wanted examples.

Our friendship began there.

Two years later he was drafted first overall and playing professional lacrosse. We were having dinner outside of One Patriot Place when I told Paul he could be a strong safety in the NFL. I thought he had the size, the speed, and the toughness to play in our league. I had a good sense of his transferrable skills because, like him, I grew up playing lacrosse.

To no surprise, he asked me countless questions and was interested in pursuing a tryout with the Patriots.

Several months later, we got on the phone to make a commitment in one direction or the other. Paul's lacrosse season was during our spring practices and that would have required him giving up lacrosse altogether. And just one week earlier, he had been named to Team USA and was scheduled to compete in the World Championships in Manchester, England, that upcoming summer.

He was at a crossroads.

I told him how rare of an opportunity it was to be able to define the pinnacle of a sport. That everything worth anything in life comes at a sacrifice. His commitment to the game of lacrosse was extraordinary, and now he would have to walk away from the game to pursue something new—something that wasn't a guarantee.

The way of the champion is not limited to the confines of a playing field. Its principles extend beyond the locker room, beyond the final whistle, into the fabric of daily life. Dedication, discipline, and the pursuit of perfection are not simply tools for success in sports, but guiding principles that can lead to greatness in any endeavor.

As you embark on this path, I encourage you to absorb the lessons within and apply them to your own pursuits, whether they be on the field, in the boardroom, or within the personal challenges we all face.

Paul ended up winning the World Championships in Manchester and taking home the Most Valuable Player recognition. And ten years later, he started the Premier Lacrosse League.

Bill Belichick

SB Champion: XXI, XXV, XXXVI, XXXVIII, XXXIX, XLIX, LI, LIII

INTRODUCTION

Every choice you make can change the trajectory of your life.

I was a twenty-four-year-old professional lacrosse player when I got a call from Bill Belichick.

Yes, the same Belichick who will finish his coaching career with the most wins and Super Bowls in NFL history. The champion of champions.

He was recruiting me to play for the Patriots.

We talked about history's most successful two-sport athletes. Antonio Gates and Julius Peppers played football and basketball. Stars like John Elway, Deion Sanders, Bo Jackson, and Russell Wilson played football and baseball. NFL Hall of Famer Jim Brown was a two-time All-American in lacrosse at Syracuse. And a few years before Belichick drafted him in the sixth round of the NFL Draft, Tom Brady had been drafted to play Major League Baseball for the Montreal Expos.

I bought pads and started working with my strength and conditioning coach on a transitional program. We were aiming at a tryout with the Patriots the following summer, just after my Major League Lacrosse season.

Then it hit me: to pursue a career in football, I had to give up lacrosse.

I'm not a quitter. Nor was I scared. But at this crossroads, I decided that turning down the opportunity was actually the harder, braver path. Making the decision to *not* play football meant that I was deciding to put everything into lacrosse. Even if it might cost me millions of dollars. Even if it might cost me a chance at winning a Super Bowl. Even if my lacrosse wage was only $15,000 a year . . . I would go all in.

This was my path.

In my second professional season, I collected my first MVP award after winning a gold medal with Team USA, yet I knew I was at only the beginning of my journey. To be good is one thing. To be great is another. To become the best there ever was? That's something worth fighting for.

I knew it would involve sacrifice. Suffering. Pain.

A relentless commitment to winning.

So I went looking for guidance. But there was no book, no road map, no blueprint that could teach me how to reach this level of ambition—how to become one of the *greatest*.

Day after day after day, I attempted to write the book myself. I had to act and choose and try and fail and then try again. I had to find teachers and mentors. I had to work. *Hard*.

One of the most valuable lessons I've learned is having the courage to ask for help. And with persistence, I built relationships with some of the greatest athletes, coaches, entertainers, and entrepreneurs in the world. I wanted to know what made them great. I even launched a podcast called *Suiting Up*, where I would interview world-class performers on their tools, tactics, and strategies for success. I wanted to know how these champions think and compete during the most critical moments of their careers—and especially when it all goes wrong.

Among many, conversations with Steph Curry, Venus and Serena Williams, Tom Brady, Abby Wambach, Mark Cuban, Dwayne Johnson, and Sue Bird taught me what I needed to know. It became clear to me that, even though every champion's path is distinct, there are recurring themes and qualities to inspire your own journey. Imagine stepping onto the field, with the weight of expectations heavy on your shoulders, and yet, embracing that pressure. Embracing it because you know that true champions thrive in adversity. They thrive because they've toiled in the shadows, perfecting their craft when no one was watching. They've honed their skills not just for the love of the game, but for the love of the process.

The Way of the Champion is not a solitary journey. It's about camaraderie, about lifting your teammates up, understanding that the collective effort yields triumph sweeter than individual accolades. It's about late-night practices that turn into early-morning drills, and the joy of feeling progress with every, sometimes painful, step forward.

In this journey, setbacks are expected. I've won and lost championships, business deals, and relationships—these are opportunities to learn from, to adapt, and to come back stronger. A champion understands that success is built upon a foundation of failures, where you choose to rise with unwavering resolve.

As we begin, let's remember that this path is not exclusive to the arena of sports. It's a philosophy that resonates through life's myriad challenges. Whether you're facing a lacrosse net, a boardroom, a classroom, or any endeavor that stirs your soul, the principles remain the same.

This book is for those who want to go *the way of the champion*.

THE WAY OF THE CHAMPION

BOOK 1 AMATEUR

Every artist was first an amateur.

—RALPH WALDO EMERSON

A *mateur* is a term that is often associated with sports, but it is really a way of being that applies to all fields. The word comes from the Latin *amator*, meaning "lover of" or "enthusiast." An amateur is someone who engages in any activity for the love of it. An amateur athlete plays for the love of the game, without the pressure of performance expectations or financial incentives. An amateur musician plays for the love of it, without the pressure of making a living at their craft. An amateur writer writes for the love of it, without concern of who, if anyone, will read their writing. The amateur is free of expectations, obligations, external pressures, and financial considerations. Here in the early stages, the goal is to find the thing you will eventually fully commit to. The thing you have *potential* in. Play different sports, try different instruments, take painting classes and acting classes and improv classes. Experiment. Be open. But always be ready to put the work in.

YOU CAN'T MISS A DAY

In the summer going into my freshman year of high school, I was at a lacrosse camp at Loyola University. Every college coach I'd ever heard of was there, from every school I'd ever seen a shirt for.

At the end of a morning session, the players packed into an auditorium for a talk from one of the all-time coaching legends and former Johns Hopkins head coach, Tony Seaman.

He began with a simple question: "Who here wants to play at a Division 1 school?"

Every kid in the room raised their hand.

"I'll tell you how to do it," he said. "And on top of it, I'll tell you how to get a full scholarship to play at a college of your choice. Who here wants a full ride?"

Every hand shot up.

"It's a simple formula," he said.

I remember feeling so present and focused on each word that it felt like I was levitating.

"There's one thing you have to do. From this day forward, through your senior year of high school," Seaman told us, "you have to shoot a hundred shots a day. That's it. You shoot a hundred shots a day from now through your senior year of high school, I guarantee you will get a full scholarship to the Division 1 college of your choice."

"Do you know how long it takes to take a hundred shots?" Seaman asked. "Thirty minutes. *Who here can find thirty minutes to take a hundred shots?*"

Every kid in the room raised their hand again.

"Here's the caveat," Seaman said. "You can't miss a day. Not a holiday. You can't miss when it's pouring down rain. You can't miss because you had a game the night before—or the day of. You can't miss a day because you're on vacation. And if you can't find a goal, make one up.

"You have to find a *way*."

I don't know about the other kids, but I walked out of that auditorium and did what Coach Seaman said. Every single day, rain or shine, I practiced. Everywhere I went, I would find a wall to throw against. A goal to shoot on. From my home state of Maryland to New York, California, and Washington, to England, Italy, Spain, Israel, and France—me, a stick, and a ball.

For twenty years.

And he was right. I was offered a full scholarship to over a dozen universities. As fortune would have it, I decided to commit to the school where Seaman had his best season as head coach—Johns Hopkins University.

It doesn't matter how ambitious or speculative the goal, you get there by taking one small step after one small step. Thirty minutes a day. One hundred shots on net, two hundred words on the page, three hundred push-ups, conditioning. Whatever reps are in your sport, in your business, in your chosen field, you do them. One after another until you hit the magic number.

And there is only one caveat:

You can't miss a day.

PUT ON YOUR BLINKERS

In the pursuit of becoming a champion, there exists a profound yet often overlooked skill: the ability to give your undivided attention.

We live in an age of constant distraction, making focus a rare gem—one that will separate you from the ordinary.

Racehorses have a field of vision that extends to 350 degrees—they can see to their left, right, and behind. That's far more than the human field of vision, which is around 180 degrees. In the late eighteenth century, a trainer named Henry Jennings began using what's called "blinkers"—a pair of small, leather screens attached to a bridle to prevent a horse from seeing anywhere but in front of them. No distractions. No concern with the competition. Focused only on their gait and the finish line.

Arguably the greatest racehorse of all time, Secretariat had a tendency to run in toward the rail during a race. In the 1970s, he ran with his famous checkered-pattern blinkers, sprinted straight, and took home the Triple Crown.

Jimmy Iovine's first job was a janitorial position at a recording studio. This was where he was introduced to the world of music production, and after dropping out of college, Iovine worked his way up from cleaner to producer. "I don't give a fuck about what anybody thinks," said the co-founder of Interscope Records and Beats by Dre. "When you're running after something, you should not look left and right . . . what does this person think, what does that person think . . . no. Go." Iovine has run after producing more than 250 albums during his career and selling Beats by Dre to Apple for $3 billion.

A champion doesn't just go through the motions. They don't allow their thoughts to drift to past victories or defeats. Rather, they eliminate the external distractions. They are wholly engaged in the present—immersing into the practice and giving it their complete focus and energy.

Feel the sweat on your brow, the strain in your muscles, the rhythm of your breath, the sound of the bass, and the ball in your stick.

Put on your blinkers.

DON'T BE AFRAID

Every year I run an event with the top fifty high school lacrosse players in the country—it's called Project 9. Each player who signs up knows that it's going to be seventy-two hours of excruciatingly hard work. There will be late-night practices and early-morning tests. Everyone has a playbook and is expected to be on time and prepared for every meeting.

It's the *scared straight* of high school lacrosse. Because like me when I was their age, very few truly know what it's like at the next level. It's fucking hard as hell, and I want them leaving the event feeling ready for it.

At the end of the weekend, I host one-on-ones. It's ten minutes of anything you want to discuss. Dialogue about lacrosse, goal setting, relationships, pressure, anxiety—anything goes.

I remember sitting with the top recruit in the nation. This kid had a heck of a motor, was insanely skilled, demonstrated great discipline, and was hungry to win at the next level. I asked him what his goals were. "I want to win a championship," he replied.

"What else?"

"Be an All-American."

"First, second, third?"

"First team."

"How many times?"

He looked at me funny.

I looked at him funny. And waited for his answer.

He said, "Maybe two-time?"

I responded, "Why not four-time?"

He said, "Yeah."

We did the same exercise with the number of national championships, what pick he would be in the Pro Lacrosse Draft, and how many gold medals he would win with Team USA.

Over my career, I've thought a lot about goal setting. Most people don't set goals because (1) the act alone is both a major and personal step in the direction of commitment, and (2) it invites hope, fear, and the possibility of regret.

I wanted to be the number-one recruit in the country. I wanted to win four national championships and become a four-time First Team All-American. I wanted to be drafted first overall in the 2008 Major League Lacrosse Draft, win ten MVPs, ten championships, and score the most points of all time. I wanted to play in four World Championships with Team USA and win four gold medals. I wanted to be the greatest ever.

I missed on most of them.

But I also did a lot more than *anyone* thought I could do.

When asked to share your most ambitious goals with someone else, you feel vulnerable. That's what this high school All-American and Player of the Year was experiencing that day.

If you don't set ambitious goals, you won't achieve ambitious things.

If you can't share them, you won't earn them.

If people think that you're crazy, the crazy ones are the ones who do it.

And in the end, if you don't reach those goals, you can carry with you the knowledge that you displayed remarkable valor, dared to tread uncharted paths, and will forever be distinguished from those who never tasted success or setback.

HERE'S THE SECRET

When people start, they want to know the secret sauce.

After Katie Ledecky won four gold medals at the Rio Summer Olympics, that's what she was asked.

And she said, "The secret is there is no secret."

Work hard.

Take care of your body—nutrition, sleep, training, recovery, and so forth.

Pay attention to the details—the little things that will add up to make a big difference.

Show up every day—whether it's a Sunday game day, a Wednesday practice day, or a Tuesday in the offseason.

Fall in love with what you do. The simplicity of it. The beauty of it. The day-to-dayness of it.

You do all of this, and on a long enough timeline, you'll get where you want to be.

EVERYONE HAS AN ORIGIN STORY

When I was twelve, my neighbor gave me his backup stick and asked me to join the local lacrosse team. Three weeks later I played my first game. Several minutes into the first quarter I took my first shot—and horribly whiffed. The ball flew backward out of my stick. My defender scooped it up, ran down the field, and scored.

But I kept at it.

Two weeks later I scored my first goal. Two years after that I was leading the county in goals as a freshman. By my senior year, I was a top 3 recruit in the country.

Often, I feel like I'm a twelve-year-old again—being introduced to a new game and starting from scratch. Most of the time I fail. Every time, I keep at it.

I think about that first shot and remind myself that it's not how you start that's important, but how you continue.

To commit. To work. To improve. To fall in love again.

UNDER THE LAMPPOST

The cofounder of the world's largest supplier of footwear and apparel, as well as a major manufacturer of sports equipment, Phil Knight, was speaking at a conference. "If you have ever run for exercise," he said to the audience, "please stand up."

Almost everyone in the room stood up.

Then he said, "If you run once a week, please stay standing. Everybody else please sit down."

There were fewer people standing.

Then he said, "If you run twice a week, please stay standing. Everybody else please sit down."

There were fewer people standing.

Then he said, "If you run more than three times a week, rain or shine, hot or cold, please stay standing. Everybody else please sit down."

Now, there were just a couple of people standing.

"Next time you're out there before the sun is up," Knight said to the couple of people still standing, "when it's dark, cold, and wet, and you're running by yourself—we are the ones standing under the lamppost, out there in the cold and wet with you, cheering you on. We're the inner athlete. We're the inner champion."

In ancient Greek philosophy and religion, the concept of the daemon refers to a divine being or guiding spirit that influences human destiny. It's an inner guiding force that helps individuals fulfill their potential and navigate the complexities of life.

Those on their way to greatness have this daemon, an inner champion that guides them. Actually, I would venture to say that *everyone* has this spirit, but not everyone listens to it—as the Nike chairman's process of elimination demonstrated.

IT'S CALLED "PLAYING"

There's not a single athlete who doesn't look back and wish they were more present. They long for those early days, when there was so much less pressure, when the stakes were lower, when life was filled with practice and friends and always getting better.

The musician Bruce Springsteen liked to say it's called "playing" music for a reason. It's called "playing" lacrosse, football, basketball, baseball, hockey, for a reason.

On the practice field, in the locker room, training in the offseason, the pregame and timeout huddles—play.

Make sure to remind yourself to have fun. Laugh. Smile. And enjoy the game.

"THAT FEELING"

In 1982, Joaquin Phoenix was an eight-year-old actor on a CBS television show called *Seven Brides for Seven Brothers*. He recalls one day on set when his friend and fellow actor, Peter Horton, was in a scene where he was in a fight with the woman who played Phoenix's mother.

He remembers watching them roll around on the ground in agony.

Despite knowing that what he was watching wasn't real, he remembers being overcome with an emotion of what was happening. He said that he was "physically buzzing" from it and it "was so fucking exciting."

Phoenix said nothing ever gives him the feeling that he gets when he's inside a special performance.

What gives you that feeling? Have you ever experienced something that's caused you to physically buzz?

It's the feeling I get when I step onto the field and look my opponent dead in the eye. The feeling of preparation and competition with a heightened sense of focus and resolve. It's the feeling I get after a grueling game where my body is completely drained and exhausted. I listen to the daemon that brings me closer to those feelings. I fight against the temptations that leave me feeling anything but.

Whatever causes you to physically buzz, well that, my friend, is worth pursuing.

FOLLOW YOUR INTERESTS

grew up with learning differences and struggled in school. So I learned to use mnemonic devices—a learning technique that helps with information retention—to pass my tests. To remember an American history lesson on the Civil War, I tied it to a play on the lacrosse field. To remember the name of a midcentury painter, I tied it to my best friend's name and hair color.

The trick worked, and eventually I made an exciting discovery about the role interest plays in memory performance. When you love the material, you're more likely to remember it.

Even now, I can recall the starting lineup of the 1993 Division 1 Champion North Carolina Tar Heels basketball team. I can pace the timing of B.J. Prager's cut and Ryan Boyle's overtime-winning assist in the 2001 Division 1 National Championship lacrosse game. I think about the first-round Eastern Conference playoff losses that the Chicago Bulls endured before Game 6 in Cleveland when Jordan hit the shot over Craig Ehlo.

From my love of the game, gradually my interests grew to include learning about the business of sport—from decades of consecutive home field sellouts at Fenway Park, to the NBA's network deal with NBC in the '90s, to Chelsea Football Club's jersey partner the season they won the Prem for the first time in eighteen years.

Memory research, dating back to the beginnings of experimental psychology, correlates with my experience. Researchers consistently find that interest facilitates memory. In fact, it's been found that memory performance is not related to education level, age, or experience. In a famous study of "good and poor readers," researchers looked at the effect of interest on recall and reading comprehension. "Good readers" read about a topic they had no interest in. "Poor readers" read about a topic they were highly interested in. The researchers found that when "poor readers" are interested in the topic, they are good readers. "On all measures," the researchers write, "children with greater [interest] recalled more than did children with less, and what they recalled was more similar to what experts recalled."

In other words, intelligence is context-dependent. As the scientist and bestselling author Angela Duckworth says, "I can be very dumb about things I don't care about and I can be extremely smart about the things I do care about."

Because I have a love for sports, launching the Premier Lacrosse League became my dream job.

Follow your interests. Look for patterns in your memories. Embedded in those memories are your interests. And embedded in those interests are the sources of your power and genius.

YOUR BLESSING IN LIFE

In his twenties, Henry Ford worked as an engineer with the Edison Illuminating Company. After a long shift, he'd go home and work on what became the Ford Motor Company.

Reflecting on these long days of constant work, Ford wrote, "I cannot say that it was hard work. No work with interest is ever hard."

One of the best things you can do is find something that you enjoy and looks like hard work to others. There was a great exchange between Jerry Seinfeld and Howard Stern:

> SEINFELD: I'm never not working on material. Every second of my existence, I'm thinking, could I do something with that?
>
> STERN: That, to me, sounds torturous.
>
> SEINFELD: Your blessing in life is when you find the torture you're comfortable with.

To Stern, what Seinfeld does sounds like torture. But Seinfeld loves what he does. And that's why he's world-class at what he does. He's found the thing that looks like hard work to others but is interesting to him.

What you love, some might find boring. But that doesn't matter. What matters is that you love that boringness, that you love what's hard, even torturous about it. I don't care what you think of lacrosse, I'm too busy thinking about all the ways it lights me up.

Your blessing in life is when you find what that is for you.

OWN THE MORNING

Every quarterback knows there is nothing better than connecting on their first throw of the game.

Every 3-point shooter knows there is nothing better than seeing their first shot of the game go through.

Every salesperson knows there is nothing better than landing a new client on the first call of the day.

And every human being knows there is nothing better than waking up and owning the morning.

Whether it's making the bed, meditating, reading, journaling, going for a run or a lift, there is no better feeling than starting the day on a win. These are what James Clear calls a "gateway habit."

Making the easy decision every morning is a gateway to making the incrementally harder decisions throughout the day.

If I start the day with that healthy act, I am more likely to want to keep it going with a healthy breakfast.

After a healthy breakfast, I am more likely to want to get a workout in.

After the workout, I'm more likely to feel good.

If I'm feeling good, I'm better at my job.

If I'm better at my job, it makes my colleagues' lives better.

And every employer knows there is nothing better than when your colleagues are happy.

For me, it all starts with a stretch and a glass of lemon water each morning.

"Your goal might be to run a marathon," Clear writes, "but your gateway habit is to put on your running shoes."

Your goal might be to own the day, but your gateway is to own the morning.

FIND YOUR DAILY PRACTICES

The artist Austin Kleon has a great line about studying the routines of productive people: "It's a wild collage of human behavior, like visiting a human zoo."

Some artists like the quiet before everyone else wakes up. Other artists like the quiet after everyone has gone to sleep. Some lacrosse players like to get their hundred shots in before they run. Others like to run, then get their hundred shots up. Some executives read to get going in the morning. Others read to wind down in the evening.

The key ingredient is routine—and flexibility. Whether I'm in a different state every week of the PLL season or I'm home in the offseason, whether the day goes smoothly or is full of surprises, whether it's a walk along a trail or around a hotel parking lot—I find the time and space for my practices.

In a world full of uncertainty, full of the unexpected, full of things we can't control, you need to find those touchstone activities. You need to find those things you can return to wherever and whenever you need to recenter, reset, refocus, or reconnect.

There is not a universal list of best daily practices. But it is universal that the best have their list of daily practices.

START IN THE PAINT

S teph Curry is known for hitting 3-pointers from well beyond the 3-point arc. So young basketball players around the world, wanting to be like Steph, practice shooting 3-pointers from well beyond the 3-point arc.

But Steph worries those kids overlook the most important thing about the way he practices: he starts in the paint, just a foot or two from the basket. His dad, the great Dell Curry, taught him this.

"Everything I did," Steph told me, "was in the paint. It was form shooting drills. It was working on mechanics because mechanics leads to confidence—when you go out [in a game] having the ball go in a bunch of times, that changes your whole mindset."

For twenty years I would begin my shooting workouts at five yards from the goal. Ten right. Ten left. Top right. Top left. Bottom right. Bottom left. Over and over.

You start close. Perfecting form, rhythm, and timing. Then you work your way out . . . once you've mastered your skill in the paint.

FOCUS ON WHAT YOU CAN CONTROL

At five feet ten, John Wooden was below average height for a basketball player. He didn't have blazing speed or Herculean strength.

However, at a young age, he recognized the importance of distinguishing between two categories: "things over which I had no control" and "things over which I had some control."

On the latter category, Wooden devoted immense intensity and effort. He dedicated himself to improving his conditioning, ball handling, and shooting skills. As a result, he achieved remarkable success during his time as a player at Purdue University, becoming the first player to earn three All-American titles.

When he graduated in 1932, Wooden's coach, Piggy Lambert, gave him high praise, calling him the best-conditioned athlete he had ever seen in any sport. Wooden attributed this to his unwavering commitment to what he could control. "I had worked at it," he said, "at what I had control over."

When he later became a coach, Wooden applied the same philosophy to his teams. He emphasized the importance of directing all efforts toward what was within their power to control.

With teams full of players focused solely on that which they could control, Wooden enjoyed one of the greatest coaching careers in the history of college basketball. In a twelve-year stretch, he led the UCLA Bruins to an incredible ten NCAA national championships, including seven consecutive titles from 1967 to 1973.

When he was inducted into the Hall of Fame as a coach in 1973, Wooden became the first individual to be enshrined as both a player and a coach.

Wooden's philosophy is also the core tenet of Stoic philosophy. The Stoic Epictetus said that the "chief task in life" is simply "to identify and separate matters, so that I can say clearly to myself which are externals not under my control, and which have to do with the choices I actually control."

One who is intensely focused on the things they can control—I don't know if I can come up with a better way to describe a true champion.

The great athletes focus on things like their training regimen, nutrition, and preparation—not the decisions of the referees, the actions of their opponents, or the people in the stands.

The great entrepreneurs focus on things like refining their products or services, developing their business strategies, and building strong relationships with customers—not economic fluctuations or market trends.

The great actors focus on things like honing their craft, their preparation for an audition or a role, and their performance on set—not how their fellow castmates perform, the preferences of critics, or the commercial success of their work.

Whether you're an actor in a play, an athlete in a game, a coach on a sideline, or an entrepreneur starting a business—focus only on what you can control.

IT'S SIMPLE MATH

When Kobe Bryant was twelve, he played a twenty-five-game basketball season without scoring a single point.

"I was terrible," he said. "Awful."

Not a single point. Not a free throw, not a lucky bounce, not a break-away layup.

When asked about that season, Kobe said it taught him to take the long view.

"I wasn't the most athletic," he said. "I had to look long term. I had to say, 'Okay, this year I'm going to get better at this. Next year, that.' And so forth and so on. And patiently, I got better."

He, like Wooden, focused on what he could control. And *patiently*, he repeats, he got better.

"It was piece by piece. It was the consistency of the work: Monday, get better. Tuesday, get better. Wednesday, get better. You do that over a period of time—three, four, five, six, seven, eight, nine, ten years—you get to where you want to go."

There are no instant experts in the game of chess, either. No overnight masters or grandmasters. There's no record of anyone—including Bobby Fischer—that indicates a person can reach grandmaster level with anything less than a decade's worth of intense practice.

Herbert Simon and William Chase drew one of the most famous conclusions in a paper in *American Scientist*: "We would estimate, very roughly, that a master has spent perhaps ten thousand to fifty thousand hours staring at chess positions."

Since you can't be working on anything for twenty-four hours a day, the question becomes, how many hours per day, on average, can you commit to your pursuit of mastery? If it's two hours a day, you'll need five thousand days—or perhaps just thirteen years, eight months, and eleven days of practice to become a master.

Kobe tells us, "It's simple math."

GET LOST IN THE PRACTICE

The entrepreneur and bestselling author Seth Godin once took a fly-fishing lesson. He asked the instructor if he had a fly without a hook. It was a strange request. What was the point? After all, you can't catch a fish without a hook.

"The next few hours were extraordinary," Godin writes. "My friends were busy trying to catch something . . . They were willing, hoping, and imploring the fish to somehow bite the hook. Relieved of this easily measured outcome, I could focus on the practice alone." He could focus solely on mastering the technique.

Of course, Godin acknowledges, at some point, you gotta bring home the fish. "But the catch is the side effect of the practice itself. Get the cast right, and the fish will be caught, or they won't."

When I was a sophomore in high school, I set a goal to develop a better left-handed shot than right. I thought it would make me a more dynamic player. So I practiced for hours and hours on net—but grew only more and more frustrated with the results. That is, until I began practicing my left-handed shot without a ball. I was no longer concerned with the outcome. It didn't matter how fast or accurate my shot was. I was able to take more reps, improve my dexterity, and create new muscle memory. Only then did I practice with a ball again.

Throughout my college and pro career, my left-handed shot had the higher scoring efficiency—rare for a righty.

Get lost in the practice. In the cast. In the shot. In mastering the technique.

You'll bring home the fish.

LET GO OF OUTCOMES

The archery master Awa Kenzo told his students to pay no attention to the target.

He would ask, what happens when an archer misses the center of the target? He would answer, "He reflects and seeks the cause of the failure within himself." And when the archer does hit the center of the target, "the sound of the arrow hitting the target should simultaneously hit the center of your being."

Success and failure come from the same place, so that's where the archer should point all of their attention: not on the outcome, but on the effort.

Don't think about making the team. Think about leaving it all out there in tryouts.

Don't think about catching the fish. Think about perfecting the cast; forget that you even have a hook.

Don't think about hitting the back of the net. Think about getting your shot off with a smooth, quick, and timely release.

Don't think about winning an Oscar. Think about your character development, the nuance and subtlety, timing and delivery of your lines.

Don't think about creating a publicly traded company. Think about the problem that needs to be solved, and the value you're creating for your customers.

Let go of the target.

THE VOICE NO ONE ELSE HEARS

Performance psychologist Jim Loehr has worked with some of the top athletes in the world. He has them wear a mic during competition and asks them to honestly articulate what the voice in their head says and thinks.

After years of this, Loehr said, "I began to realize what really matters in a really significant way is the tone and the content of the voice no one else hears. I came to understand that the ultimate coach for all of us in life is that private voice. And that private voice can be brutal—a detriment to being the best you can be, a detriment to your happiness, and a detriment to a sense of satisfaction."

Almost invariably, Loehr said, our negative thought pattern shows up in the same or similar situations. For a tennis player, it might be when they double-fault for the second or third time. For a salesperson, it might be when they get hung up on for the umpteenth time. For a writer, it might be when they've been in a Google doc for two hours and have but a paragraph to show for it.

The way to break a negative thought pattern? Be prepared with a positive one. So in practice, Loehr would have that tennis player write down what she *should* say to herself when she double-faults for the second or third time. Instead of "My serve is so bad today," it might be "I always get my serve back on track." Or the salesperson—instead of "I'm terrible at selling," it might be "Each call is getting me closer to a sale!"

Whatever the circumstances, Loehr said the rule of thumb he uses is to ask, *Is this how I would speak to someone I deeply care about?* Or, *If I were speaking to someone I deeply cared about, what would I say to them?*

Athletes are not machines. We're emotional beings capable of fear and confidence. When your team starts to gain momentum, there's a distinct shift in your attitude and performance. You begin to believe you can win.

Think about some of your negative thought patterns. We all have them. And then, find a better alternative.

Momentum carries with itself a dual nature. Understanding the psychological underpinnings and their influence on your performance can be the difference in winning and losing.

CULTIVATE RANGE

You will be pushed to sport-specialize. The logic will be compelling. If you play a sport year-round, you'll acquire skills faster, be better at an earlier age, and therefore be more likely to get recruited to play at the next level.

Don't take the bait.

Coming out of high school, my college teammate was considered one of the best lacrosse players in the country—a status he carried since middle school. But he only ever played lacrosse.

As I got better and better in college, and well into the pros, I noticed that I was tapping into skills I picked up playing basketball, soccer, and track and field. I kept adding to my lacrosse game. On the other hand, that teammate's abilities hit a ceiling. And as a result, he didn't improve, and lost his starting spot on the team.

Instead of going all in on one sport, cultivate what the great sports science writer David Epstein calls *range*. "What we see in the development of elite athletes," Epstein says, "is that they sample a bunch of sports early on and only later do they specialize."

With range, you have a higher ceiling.

There was a cool study of the development paths of 102 German soccer players. Eighteen of them made the national team that won the 2014 World Cup. The others didn't make it beyond the top amateur league. There was one key difference in their development paths. The future World Cup–winning national team members, the researchers write, "participated more frequently in non-organized leisure play than organized practice/training" and had "more engagement in other sports in adolescence . . . and more organized [practice] only in adulthood."

Not to mention . . . specialization is exhausting.

Michael Phelps is an inspiring cautionary tale for all of us. His singular focus on swimming is what made him the best in the world, but then, it's also what made him walk away from the sport before his time. It was only when he'd balanced his life a bit that he was able to find the drive and passion to compete again. Former NFL quarterback Andrew Luck has a similar story: he announced his shocking early retirement in part because of how "empty" he felt having dedicated nearly everything in his life to a single pursuit.

Freely play—without structure and organization—many sports. Play the long game. Raise your ceiling. Cultivate range.

ADAPT AND ADVANCE

Growing up, Rudy Cline-Thomas wanted to play basketball at the highest level. Larry Bird was his idol. But in the fall of his junior year at Providence College, Rudy accepted that playing basketball at the highest level wasn't in his future. So he began to let go of his dream of playing in the NBA. He began thinking of how he might be able to channel his love of basketball into other avenues.

Rudy went to his college counseling office. There he was shown a binder full of addresses and contacts for companies with internship opportunities. Rudy wrote down the addresses and contact information for two of them: Reebok and the NBA. Then he went home and applied for internships at both.

A week later, Rudy got good news from Reebok. He had been accepted to work the following summer at their six-story headquarters in Stoughton, Massachusetts. After he read the acceptance letter, Rudy didn't feel excited. That surprised him. But he knew what it meant: he wanted the NBA internship.

Rudy put down the Reebok letter and then wrote one to the NBA just to reemphasize his interest in the internship position. A week later, he wrote another one. A week after that, another one. For weeks and weeks, Rudy heard nothing from the NBA. So as his junior year was coming to a close, Rudy finalized plans to move to Stoughton.

"Two days before the end of my junior year," Rudy told me, "the NBA called me."

Someone who had initially accepted an internship with the NBA that summer decided to pull out.

"I was the last person that they let into the program," Rudy said. "When I later spoke to the coordinator of the internship program, she told me that by not giving up, her getting all those letters consistently, is what got me in there."

That type of persistence didn't stop. Neither did the handwritten letters.

One of the perks of that summer internship was access. Rudy wrote letters on personal stationery to every single NBA agent. Before the summer ended, Rudy secured a postgrad job at one of the top law firms in the nation, Williams & Connolly, where he became the youngest agent in the NBA.

In his book *Mastery*, Robert Greene writes about "the adaptation strategy." Sometimes, the road we first want to go down isn't meant to be. Rudy wanted to play in the NBA. But he had to face the reality: he wasn't good enough to play in the NBA. He could have spent years mourning the death of a dream. He could have abandoned the game he loved entirely. He could have held on to the glory days, being the king of his high school basketball team.

But instead, Rudy adapted. He took what he had cultivated through playing basketball—his love and knowledge of the game, his ability to understand and work with athletes, his persistence and creativity—and went in a new direction.

After announcing his retirement in 2023, four-time NBA champion and 2015 NBA Finals MVP Andre Iguodala began his next gig running a $200 million venture capital fund with longtime friend, agent, and business partner Rudy Cline-Thomas.

"You don't want to abandon the skills and experience you have gained," Greene writes, "but to find a new way to apply them. Your eye is on the future, not the past. Often such creative readjustments lead to a superior path."

BE COACHABLE

Not all work ethic is created equal. If you're sailing in the wrong direction, you're sailing against the wind. I've seen extremely hard workers funnel their effort into the wrong things.

Plenty of talented athletes don't make the cut. Plenty of talented athletes don't find their edge.

The way you get an edge, Bill Belichick told me, "is by being coachable." Belichick has seen plenty of talent come in and out of the NFL. He's seen plenty of highly touted draft picks become one-and-done busts. He's seen plenty of undrafted free agents become stars. He's seen the 199th pick become the greatest quarterback of all time.

"My experience has been," Belichick said, "an athlete who listens to the coaching and then goes out and works hard, they improve. If they don't listen to the coaching, if they go out and work hard but they do it their way—they work but it's not productive work—they don't improve. And if they listen to the coaching, but they don't work hard—they don't improve, either."

The same goes for business. I asked a former business colleague of mine, who has recently scaled the ranks at several Fortune 500 companies, what's the secret? He told me it's all about being coachable—and well liked. Which is a derivative of kindness and hard work.

Being coachable is being curious and eager. It's being self-aware and ambitious.

Tom Brady was very coachable. "He wasn't all that good when we got him," Coach Belichick said. "He mechanically wasn't anywhere near where he eventually ended up. . . . He's worked hard on his throwing mechanics. He's earned everything that he's achieved."

JaMarcus Russell was the first overall pick in the 2007 NFL Draft. He was resistant to feedback, and as a result, his performance didn't elevate to the level needed to maintain a spot on an NFL roster. He was cut after just three seasons in the league. The divergence of Russell's and Brady's careers speaks for itself.

Talent is a commodity. Work ethic is a commodity. But the ability to take coaching and instruction, to hear a critique and then work to address it—that is rare.

Be rare. Be coachable.

THE NEXT BEST PLAY

When we make a mistake, we often come up with an excuse.

Especially when we've practiced extraordinarily hard, prepared, and still come up short.

North Carolina Hall of Fame coach Dean Smith was an expert in teaching accountability.

When his players made a mistake, he would tell them they must "recognize it, admit it, learn from it, and forget it." That's how you put yourself in the best position to get the next one.

When I think about the games I played poorly in—and there were *a lot*—the primary source of consecutive turnovers and bad decisions was my inability to forget the previous one. In lacrosse, we go through shooting slumps, much like how hitters in baseball go through a version of their own.

Coach Smith said that the most often skipped-over step was admitting the mistake. Probably because, as athletes, we feel weak when we own our faults.

If we can't admit to our mistake, we can't learn. If we can't learn, we can't forget. And if we can't forget, we can't make the next best play.

THE THREE MONKEYS

The metaphorical three monkeys are adopted worldwide as a message of peace and tolerance.

Hear no evil, see no evil, speak no evil.

We should practice that in life and sport.

Phil Jackson was one of the greatest coaches in NBA history. Over his career he led his teams to thirteen championships—two as a player and eleven as a coach. He did it by motivating his team to find success both on the court and in life.

"Once you've done the mental work, there comes a point you have to throw yourself into the action and put your heart on the line. That means not only being brave but being compassionate towards yourself, your teammates and your opponents."

There are many moments in sport where we can fall into the trap of blame—lacking compassion for our teammates after a simple turnover, shitty first half, or playoff loss. You might turn to criticize a teammate who didn't play their best, or question the coach's game plan.

No matter the moment, the only way forward is through accountability and acceptance, courage and encouragement, optimism and belief.

Especially in your own locker room, the three monkeys will serve as tolerance for the team.

THE GOLDEN MEAN

The Greek philosopher Aristotle said that all virtues are in between two vices.

This is now known as the "golden mean" or the "Doctrine of the Mean." Courage is between cowardice and recklessness. Confidence is between self-doubt and arrogance. Hard work is between being lazy and being a workaholic.

We have to remember that as ambitious, driven, talented people, there is a catch-22 to all that we do, and it can be taken too far. It's easier to worry about not doing enough, not going hard enough, not pushing through enough.

But we also have to keep our eye on when our courage "overleaps itself" and lands firmly into the category of recklessness. When our discipline is taken too far and leads to burnout. When our confidence and the belief in our own abilities tip over to selfishness and the inability to be coached.

Finding the golden mean, finding the right amount, is an art. It takes a lot of practice, experimentation, and study to figure out the right amount of the right thing at the right time.

A WEEK OFF IS REALLY TWO

Vince Vaughn estimates that he got hired after one in every *one thousand* auditions when he was starting out as an actor. He got rejected for roles in *Friends, Dazed and Confused, Donnie Darko,* and *There's Something about Mary*—to name a few.

At first, he struggled with this, as anyone would. People were telling him that he wasn't right, that he couldn't do it, that they didn't believe in him. Over and over and over again.

"I would get down," Vaughn said. "I would take a week, and I would just not do anything. I'd lose my energy." The problem became a vicious cycle—down on losing the job, on being rejected, he wouldn't attend classes, practice monologues, or even watch movies. All things that he knew would help his craft.

"But then I started to realize," he said, "that the week I took off was really two weeks. It was a week of not getting better *and* it was a week of getting worse. Two weeks less of improving at the things I'm in control of."

After realizing that a week off is really two, Vaughn began to accept that rejections are just part of it. He'd get rejected for a role, wake up the next day, and get back to working on his craft—trusting that if he kept improving, the auditions-to-rejections ratio would get smaller and smaller.

Look, the path to success, the path you are on—it's going to be riddled with failures and rejections and mistakes and losses and bad games and bad seasons. All the greats—athletes, actors, entrepreneurs, *all* of them—have their own long list of failures.

Shooting 30 percent from the field is considered top-class in the PLL. That means that you're failing to score on seven out of every ten attempts. Missing your shot is just part of it.

So a dividing line between success and failure is simply the ability to bounce back quickly. To accept that failure is part of this process. And never mope just because you messed up, never take a week off. Because it's really two.

GET THE EXTRA MINUTES

I t might take ten thousand hours to master a skill. It might take more. There is no scenario in which it does not take a lot of hours and reps.

"Here's the thing," two-time Olympic gold medalist and World Cup alpine skier Mikaela Shiffrin said, "most of the time on the mountain, I'm not skiing downhill." There's the time on the chairlift. The time on flat cat tracks. The time standing still listening to the coach's instructions and feedback.

To get her ten thousand hours, Shiffrin explained, "I always practice, even on the cat tracks or in those interstitial periods." In other words, even when she's just stopping, she's sure to do it right. Even in the lift line, she's sure to maintain a good position. Even when she's not on snow, she's sure to be thinking about counter-rotational force. "Consider that thirty seconds that all the others spend just straight-lining from the bottom of the race-course to the bottom of the lift," she said. "I use that part to work on my turns. I'm getting extra minutes."

When I would walk across campus from one class to the next, I would envision myself dodging opponents on the way to the goal. Every student coming toward me was a defender closing space. I would think about the timing and footwork of every jab-step and hesitation move I'd use in a game. These were small, mental reps that were additive to practice. I always thought about the game. I wanted every edge that I could get—even if that meant dodging undergrads in the Johns Hopkins quad.

Great bands release maybe seven albums over the course of a career. You don't become a great musician just by making albums. How else would the first few be good?

Great writers publish maybe half a dozen books. You don't become a great writer just by publishing books.

Great entrepreneurs start three companies. You don't become a great entrepreneur just by starting companies.

You gotta find those interstitial periods to get your reps. You have to use this time right now, *before* you are on the big stage, before you've turned pro, to practice and learn and grow. Those moments between moments.

The time is now, here in the early stages, before anyone is looking. When nobody cares. When nobody notices. Get the extra minutes.

THE ASSASSIN'S CREED

t's not going to be easy to become a champion. It requires as much strength and speed as it does endurance.

The truth is, to achieve greatness, you need to have the mindset of a trained assassin. You have to be willing to do whatever it takes to win. That's the way the math works. One team wins, the other team loses. One fighter stands, the other falls. You should be ruthlessly ambitious, and then, learn how to control it.

Before every game, Michael Jordan would find his motivation. Or he'd create it out of thin air. With the best record in NBA history and on the Chicago Bulls' way to their fifth NBA title, Jordan needed to find "it" against the Seattle Supersonics ahead of Game 1 of the 1996 Finals. The night before the game, Supersonics head coach George Karl walked past him in a restaurant and didn't say hello. "He walked right past me," Jordan said. "I said [to myself], 'that's a crock of shit. . . . You gonna do this? Fine.' That's all I needed. That's all I needed was for him to do that, and it became personal with me."

Jordan went out and *torched* the Supersonics.

After winning Game 2 of the first round of the 2023 NBA playoffs, Memphis Grizzlies' forward Dillon Brooks called LeBron James "old." The next game, LeBron put up 22 points and 22 rebounds—his first time going 20 and 20 in the playoffs. The Lakers won in six, and after being bounced from the playoffs in a 40-point blowout, Brooks didn't show up to his post-game media interview and was fined $25,000.

One of the winningest and most decorated coaches in European football history, Pep Guardiola, described Lionel Messi as not human. "He's an animal," he said. "When he passes the ball, he attacks the goal like a machine. He can smell the goal." The record eight-time Ballon d'Or Messi is on a permanent quest to win, and it's impossible to change his mentality.

With 39 major titles and a record 367 career wins, Serena Williams said, "Life was get up, six o'clock in the morning, go to the tennis court before school. . . . I hate to put it [like this] but it's like training an animal." Intimidation was part of her repertoire.

Shared stories from Cristiano Ronaldo's teammates revolve around his tenacity. "Training with him was like a war," said former Manchester United forward and Bulgarian national team player, Dimitar Berbatov. "He came early and was in the gym. Then he stayed late to practice against a goalkeeper. He then ended up going for a swim before heading back to the gym. He was determined to be the best."

Michael and LeBron and Messi and Serena and Cristiano are assassins. They're not friendly, kindly people—not when they're playing anyway. You provoke them at your peril.

You can be a nice guy off the court, but if you want to be a champion, you're going to need intimidation. When you get to the very top, you'll find that those who are up there with you have the same focus, qualities, and practices. The dividing line then becomes one of mentality. And you've got to be a killer, the guy that people point to and say, "Damn, he's a *motherfucker*."

There's an old expression from Japanese philosopher, Miyamoto Musashi. It goes like this: "It's better to be a warrior in a garden than a gardener at war."

To be *the* champion, you need to take the assassin's creed.

FIND YOUR GUYS

For everybody who makes it, there is somebody who was way more talented but didn't. It's a sad fact of life. There are many reasons for it—luck, timing, privilege. We don't need to speculate on all that because so much of it is outside a person's control.

But one reason is both simple and up to us.

Success is so often a product of who we know and who influences us.

"Show me who you spend time with," Johann Wolfgang Goethe once said, "and I will show you who you are."

I've seen enough top draft picks get cut to confidently add to this quote: "The type of people you spend most of your time with will determine your success."

That's exactly what comedian and actor Marc Maron often asks other successful artists: *Who were your guys? Who did you come up with? Who was in your class?* Almost everyone was or is part of a cohort of other comedians and performers. They pushed one another, motivated and encouraged one another. Maron asks these questions because he almost didn't make it. He got caught up with the wrong crowd at The Comedy Store, became addicted to drugs with the late actor and comedian, Sam Kinison—setting his career back by years.

You find a scene that makes you better and you'll get better. You find one that sucks you down, you'll circle the drain together.

It doesn't have to be in-person, either. Cumulatively, I spent more time reading about and listening to the greatest athletes and entrepreneurs through autobiographies and podcasts than I did hanging with friends in the lunch hall.

Find your people. Find the *right* people.

WATCH FILM

Academy Award–winning filmmaker Quentin Tarantino didn't attend film school. Instead, he obsessively studied the careers of great filmmakers—so much so, it is said, that he could write many of their biographies.

"Whether it be Brian De Palma or Howard Hawks or Douglas Sirk or Martin Scorsese or whoever," he said, "I was very interested in following directors' careers and studying them and the evolution of their careers . . . I would just obsess about filmmakers the way a big baseball fan would obsess about their favorite baseball players."

For me it was lacrosse. Growing up, I had a TV and VHS player set up next to my bed and every night, I watched lacrosse until I fell asleep. Back in high school, there wasn't YouTube . . . hardly any DVDs. There were so few games on TV that I ended up watching the same four VHS tapes I had on loan from my assistant coach on repeat, over and over.

There were three midfielders who stood out to me in those four tapes: Jay Jalbert (UVA), Josh Sims (Princeton), and A.J. Haugen (Johns Hopkins). I like to think there are skills that each possessed that I practiced in the backyard, envisioning what it would be like to be a combination of the three.

Jay Jalbert stood for agility, toughness, and creativity at the position. He was shifty and strong. He dodged straight into the teeth of the defense. He was great off the ground and loved scrapping between the lines. He could pass and shoot on the run.

Josh Sims ran like a deer. He patented the "downhill dodge." It was fast. He made it look easy. He used both hands equally. And his shot came overhand, sidearm, and underhand.

A.J. Haugen's shooting on the run was pure art. Everything was precise. It always came overhand, shoulder cocked back, following through right off his ear. He would hide his release from the goalie and always put the ball off hip—the hardest place for a goalie to get to. I would watch him shoot, then practice it in my backyard. Rinse and repeat.

These days, there's so much content out there. You can watch highlights of great athletes on YouTube, games on demand, and so forth. You can watch entrepreneurs pitching investors on *Shark Tank*. You can watch documentaries on the icons of nearly every industry across any major streaming platform.

Athletes and entrepreneurs are more like chemists than they are inventors. They take the best practices of learned success and meld them into something new.

What do you want to accomplish, and who do you aspire to be like? Go study them. Watch film. Take notes. Practice doing the things they did.

That's what I did. That's what I'm still doing today—every night reviewing film before bed.

STUDY THE PEOPLE WHO SHOULDN'T BE GOOD

The bestselling author and hit podcast host Tim Ferriss has a great rule for learning anything faster: study the people who shouldn't be as good as they are.

Don't study the running back who is built like a truck *and* runs a 4.3-second 40-yard dash. Study the undersized running back with average speed who somehow made it to the league and won multiple Super Bowls.

Don't study the actor with conventional good looks and a privileged background who landed a leading role in their first audition. Study the actor who faced rejection after rejection, struggled to make ends meet, and worked tirelessly to perfect their craft before finally achieving success in their career.

Don't study the entrepreneur with a wealthy family background and practically unlimited resources who started a successful business. Study the entrepreneur who faced financial struggles, bootstrapped their venture, and encountered numerous failures before ultimately building a thriving company.

That's what Joel Embiid did. He lived in the gym and he watched a lot of videos on the internet.

Embiid was born in Cameroon, and at the age of sixteen, he got recruited to play high school basketball in Florida. He had been playing basketball for only three months at that point. He was big and could dunk, but that was about it. He couldn't handle the ball. He couldn't pass. He couldn't shoot.

"So I went to the practice on the first day," Embiid wrote, "and I was so bad that the coach kicked me out of the gym. I didn't know what I was doing."

The other kids made fun of how bad he was. Embiid said they were like those bullies in the movies. And that unlocked Embiid's competitiveness.

43

He decided he was going to work and work until he was good, until those kids had nothing to make fun of.

He started staying after practice to get extra shots. He dribbled a basketball everywhere he went. And as for shooting, Embiid explained, "I'm chilling one night, and I go on YouTube, and I'm thinking I'm about how to figure this shooting thing out." Initially, he searched tips on shooting 3-pointers and form, but he didn't find what he was looking for. Eventually, he had an idea. Embiid typed in: "white people shooting 3-pointers."

"I know it's a stereotype," said Embiid, "but have you ever seen a normal, 30-year-old white guy shoot a three-pointer? That elbow is tucked, man. The knees are bent. The follow-through is perfect. Always." So, Embiid learned from watching random people on YouTube. "Those are the guys I learned from," he says. "Just random people shooting threes with perfect form."

Then at practice and in games, he would try to imitate how they shot the ball. "I started being able to compete," he said. "It was crazy, because getting some range changed my whole game."

A couple of years later, Embiid committed to Kansas. After a year at Kansas, he was drafted third overall by the Philadelphia 76ers in the 2014 NBA Draft. And in 2023, Joel Embiid was the NBA MVP.

STICK WITH IT

To fill time in his stand-up routine, in 1963, comedian Steve Martin decided to try to learn an instrument.

For no particular reason, Martin chose the banjo. He bought a book called *How to Play the 5-string Banjo*, by Pete Seeger. The first lesson was how to strum a C chord. When Martin strummed a C chord, "I couldn't tell the difference," he admitted. To him, when he strummed a C chord, it sounded just like when he strummed without touching any strings.

"But I just stayed with it," he said. "And I kept telling myself, 'Well, if I just stay with it, one day, I will have played for forty years.' Anybody who sticks with [the banjo] for forty years will be able to play it."

Martin stayed with it, and in 2001, he won a Grammy for Best Country Instrumental Music Performance. It took thirty-eight years, one day at a time, staying with it.

When it gets tough, remind yourself that eventually the minutes and hours will add up.

Stick with it. Be patient.

A LITTLE BIT BETTER

Tom Brady loves winning. This is why he breaks golf clubs. This is why he breaks tablets. This is why he screams at his teammates and coaches.

But, early on, it wasn't that obsession with winning that set in motion the future greatest of all time. Early on, it was an obsession with getting a little bit better each day.

"He taught himself to love the feeling of improvement," Seth Wickersham writes in *It's Better to Be Feared*. "He taught himself to love the feeling of finishing the day with the knowledge that he was a little bit better."

Continual incremental improvement is the gateway to success. Instead of focusing on winning, focus on

> . . . improving your stick skills a little bit.
> . . . improving your shooting accuracy a little bit.
> . . . improving your strength and conditioning a little bit.
> . . . improving your ability to perform under pressure a little bit.
> . . . improving your ability to rebound after a bad play a little bit.

In the beginning, these efforts don't look like they are amounting to much. That's why most people don't focus on the little things. That's why most people don't learn to love small improvements. That's why most people aren't Tom Brady.

At the time of this writing, Warren Buffett was the fifth-wealthiest person on the planet. He's famously said, "My life has been a product of compound interest."

Buffett's incredible wealth is a product not so much of his investing abilities, but of his time in the game.

In its simplest form, compound interest accrues on both the money you save and the interest you earn. Year over year, it multiplies. One line of math would indicate that if you put aside five dollars per day into an account with an 8 percent return, it would turn into over one million bucks in fifty years.

Compound interest is one of the most powerful forces on earth. And you can apply that to . . .

Your skills
Your health
Your nutrition
Your sleep
Your craft
Your career
Your knowledge
Your relationships

Remember, the key to harnessing the power of compound interest is consistency and long-term commitment. The number-one rule of compounding, they say, is to not interrupt.

Keep making those small, incremental efforts.

It's pretty simple: getting a little bit better every day compounds over time to make you the greatest.

ALL SUCCESS IS A LAGGING INDICATOR

In the documentary *Free Solo*, there's a scene where a team of neuroscientists perform an MRI and conclude that the climber Alex Honnold's brain abnormally responds to fear stimuli.

"I find that irritating," Honnold later said. "I've spent twenty-five years conditioning myself to work in extreme conditions, so of course my brain is different—just as the brain of a monk who has spent years meditating or a taxi driver who has memorized all the streets of a city would be different."

To be sure, Honnold experiences fear. But fear informs his planning. For instance, before he climbed El Capitan—a three-thousand-foot rock wall in Yosemite—without a rope, "I'd drive into Yosemite, look at the wall, and think, 'No way. Too scary.'" So he climbed El Cap more than fifty times *with* a rope.

Fear and preparation are inversely proportional. The level of fear "depends [on] the level of preparation," Honnold says. When he feels confident, the confidence is a lagging indicator of the previous prep work put in.

Heisman trophy winner Joe Burrow was the first overall selection in the 2020 NFL Draft. Before his NFL Training Camp premiere, ESPN anchor Dan Patrick asked him if he had any doubts. Burrow said, "No. Why would I?" His confidence comes from preparation. "I win the games on Monday, Tuesday, Wednesday, and Thursday. I don't win them on Saturday." He knew the NFL was going to be really hard. He also knew that he was going to work harder than any other player in the league. That was his commitment to the game. His commitment to himself.

A lot of our best moments in life are a product of the previous work put in. When you're shooting the ball well, that's a lagging indicator of countless hours spent practicing in the backyard. A golfer's smooth swing is a lagging indicator of thousands of swings taken. A quarterback throwing sixty touchdowns in a season is a lagging indicator of hundreds of touchdowns thrown in practice.

Becoming fluent in a foreign language is a lagging indicator of consistent practice and dedication. Graduating with honors from university is a lagging indicator of persistent studying and academic excellence. Running a successful marathon is a lagging indicator of months of rigorous training.

Winning a championship, selling a company, achieving financial independence, building strong and fulfilling relationships—all success is a lagging indicator.

YOU ARE ON A DIFFERENT PATH

During a windy practice in high school, Tom Brady's receivers weren't catching the ball. Maybe the wind was making it difficult to judge the ball's trajectory, so Brady tried throwing harder. Didn't work. They were just bad receivers. After practice, Brady was pissed and went to tell his coach as much.

"You need to be more patient," Brady's coach told him.

"Look around at everybody else on this field. You know what? There's a very good chance that in ten years from now, everybody else on this field will no longer be playing. You're still going to be playing."

At some point, you will experience the impatience of the talented. You will get pissed at teammates who can't catch the ball. You will get pissed at teammates for not putting in the extra work with you after practice. You will get pissed at yourself for poor play. And it will be hard.

Know that you will be playing for a long time. Do a few dropped passes during a windy high school practice really matter? No. Be patient—with your teammates, with coaches, with yourself.

STOP AND TAKE THE PEBBLE OUT

Ross Edgley is an assassin.

He climbed the height of Mount Everest on a rope . . . in one attempt. He ran a marathon . . . with a car strapped to his back. He completed a triathlon . . . with a hundred-pound tree on his back. He swam sixty-two miles in the Caribbean . . . with a hundred-pound log tied to him. And he was the first person in history to swim all the way around Great Britain, all 1,792 miles of it over the course of 157 grueling, awful days in the water.

You might think Ross has cultivated the ability to endure anything and put up with everything. You might think he is the type to grit his teeth and bear it all. To an extent, he is, but only with things that are unavoidable and out of his control. Otherwise, he doesn't needlessly suffer.

He defines resilience as *suffering strategically managed*, which he elaborates on with an example: "If you are running a marathon and you have a pebble in your shoe—resilience isn't continuing to run, grinding the pebble into the ground. No, you stop and take the pebble out of your shoe and then continue on."

Winning isn't done with brute force. It doesn't always hurt. Yes, the champion is resilient. But not in the foolish, grind the pebble into the ground kind of way. Champions don't needlessly suffer. They listen to feedback—from their coaches and their bodies. They refine and make changes. They stop and take the pebble out of their shoe.

RUN THROUGH THE LINE

Every coach in the world has said it. On the lacrosse field, the football field, the basketball court, the volleyball court, the tennis court, the hockey rink. It doesn't matter what surface you play on, you've heard a coach say . . .

Run through the line.

Why? Why does it actually matter? What's the difference between running through the line and easing up a few feet in front of the line?

In a 2000 study, Peter Weyand, director of the SMU lab, working with a team at Harvard, determined that elite sprinters gained maximum speed by striking the ground with a greater force than others in relation to their body weight, and for a shorter period of time. It's called peak impact force.

In the case of the fastest human being on the planet, Usain Bolt, his peak impact force can surpass one thousand pounds.

Peak impact force is delivered within three-hundredths of a second, or thirty milliseconds, of striking the ground. It is the most crucial moment in sprinting. It's so crucial that Laurence Ryan, a physicist in the SMU lab, called this period "30 milliseconds to glory."

If thirty milliseconds leads to glory, don't pull up at the end and lose the race.

THE LITTLE THINGS

Hustling in and out of substitutions, winning a team sprint during practice, grabbing the balls out of the cage and lining them up for the next shooting drill, being the first in line, making eye contact with your coach in huddles, never walking during practice or games . . .

We focus on the little things because they're not so little.

John Wooden would teach his athletes how to put their socks and shoes on right.

My college coach Dave Pietramala's mantra was to "do the little things."

Every missed assignment and inaccurate shot are caused by a fraction of a second delay or slightly misjudged angle on release. If we put our best effort into the little things going our way, we're going to win more fractions of a second and better angles. It's being obsessed with the details of your assignment.

Little things set the right tone for yourself and your teammates. They're contagious. A team with a culture of doing the little things end up winning the biggest thing.

BE GREAT EVERYWHERE

One of the things I look for in sport and business is how someone handles the stuff other people think doesn't matter. Lots of people are good at what the crowd cheers for. They work hard at the stuff that's rewarding, fun, and easy to notice.

Biographer David Halberstam wrote that what set Bill Belichick apart from other young coaches was that "he wanted the grunt work." The sign of a coach who won't do great things, Halberstam wrote, is that they put more effort into the stuff that has the glory, that gets noticed and applauded. Belichick, on the other hand, "understood that the key to success, the secret to it, was the mastery of the grunt work, all the little details."

Coach Pietramala—the only person in lacrosse history to have won Player of the Year, Coach of the Year, and a Division 1 National Championship as a player and a head coach—would tell me, "character is what you do when nobody is watching." Picking up every ball after practice, turning in your homework on time, showing up early to meetings, picking up a piece of trash on the ground that you notice on your walk to class, holding the door for your neighbor at the local restaurant. The grunt work. The champion's work.

What distinguishes the greatest from the merely great is that the greatest don't turn it on and off. They are wedded to certain behaviors and habits. They do them all the time. They strive for greatness every day, everywhere, on and off the field.

DISCOVER HOW YOU LEARN BEST

'm a visual learner. There's a reason for this.

I grew up with auditory processing disorder (APD). Basically, I had to read the material two to three times to understand the content. I processed information slower than other students did. But because of APD, I was given note-taking support, extra time on exams, and access to my school's tutoring programs—all very helpful.

However, by virtue of my challenges in the classroom, I would resort to other creative and visual ways to learn.

My short- and long-term memory was sharp. I was strong with numbers and excelled in art class. I found I absorbed much more information when I watched and listened, rather than read. That's why I spent a dozen hours in a studio reading this book into a mic so it could be available to those who prefer to listen.

Wayne Gretzky watched the NHL on TV and studied where his favorite players liked to be on the ice. Serena Williams said she was a "tactile learner" and needed the physical repetitions and more hands-on experiences. Michael Phelps was big on visualization—in his mind's eye, he would watch the "videotape" of the perfect race before bed every night.

Everyone learns differently. The key is discovering how you best learn.

Bullying and peer pressure can hold significant space in each of our lives—especially as amateurs. It turned out that my learning difference, which at the time made my classwork challenging, also became a reinforcing mechanism for how I practiced:

Always two to three times more than my competitors. That's how I learned.

Harness your unique learning style. What appears as an inability might become your greatest asset in mastering your chosen field.

EVERY DAY IS A GIFT

G rowing up, George Lucas wanted to be a race car driver or a car mechanic. He was obsessed with cars, car garages, and working on his yellow Fiat Bianchina.

But then, Lucas was nearly killed in a car accident.

He was rushed to the hospital, and several hours later, he woke up with an oxygen tube in his nose and a needle in his arm where a blood transfusion was underway.

He would spend the next four months in bed recovering—and thinking.

"I realized more than anything else what a thin thread we hang on in life," Lucas said, "and I really wanted to make something out of my life."

It was an accident he shouldn't have survived. The racing belt he had carefully installed himself failed. It snapped, so Lucas was ejected from the car before it rolled into a tree.

"So it was like, 'Well, I'm here, and every day now is an extra day. I've been given an extra day so I've got to make the most of it.' . . . You can't help in that situation but get into a mindset like that. . . . You've been given this gift and every single day is a gift. And I wanted to make the most of it."

After the accident, he said, "[I began] to apply myself at school. I got great grades . . . and eventually discovered film and film schools."

You don't need to be in a near-fatal car accident to get shook into the "every single day is a gift" mindset that fueled Lucas to make the Star Wars franchise.

The thought of our mortality shouldn't create panic. It should create clarity and a sense of urgency. The realization that life hangs on a thin thread, that each day is a gift, that we are not on this planet for very long, can be an incredibly motivating force. It reminds us to be intentional, to seek opportunities for growth and self-discovery, and to make a positive impact on the world around us while we can. Let us embrace each day with gratitude, purpose, and determination, and like George Lucas, make the most of the extraordinary gift of life.

DON'T DAYDREAM

Arnold Schwarzenegger said having a vision without setting goals is just daydreaming.

You have to know not only what you're trying to do, but how to measure whether you're accomplishing it.

Each of us takes on two important things on our journey to becoming a champion.

First is, yeah, those big dreams. Dream as big as you possibly can—picture what it would look like to be the greatest ever at your sport. The impact it would have on you, your family, friends, colleagues, and industry.

Next is knowing all the effort, the suffering, and the fulfillment that the journey would entail. Setting concrete goals and benchmarks—all marks you'll have to hit if you want to get there.

No one becomes a champion overnight. They start by setting goals. They start with one hundred shots a day. They start by making the team. They start by winning the first game of the season. They put the goal through the goalposts . . . and then they move those goalposts over and over again until they end up somewhere no one else thought was possible.

Dream big. Set goals. Work hard every day.

KNOW YOUR COMPETITION BETTER THAN THEY KNOW THEMSELVES

When I showed up at Johns Hopkins, I was highly touted as an offensive player. Yet my college coach is considered one of the all-time great defensive players.

In my first few months on campus, Coach Pietramala made me play defense. It was frustrating. *Fuck this,* I remember frequently thinking, *I was brought here to score goals, not help prevent them.*

Petro must have sensed my frustration. "I don't let any player on this team play offense," he told me, "until they learn my defense. Because what happens when you're on the field and you get stuck on defense? I can't run the risk of you not knowing what to do."

I didn't start playing offense at Hopkins until I mastered his defensive schemes.

Take note from Peyton Manning and Ray Lewis: both preach being a student of the other side of the ball. Manning would say he knows the linebacker position better than most linebackers. Lewis would say he knows the quarterback position better than most quarterbacks. Because Manning's job as a quarterback was to read the linebacker and Lewis's job as a linebacker was to read the quarterback, their understudying of the opposite position helped them become better players.

During overtime of the 2005 Division 1 National Semifinal, I tracked back on defense against the Virginia Cavaliers. We got a stop and reverse transitioned to the other end—where I ended up making the game-winning assist to Benson Erwin, a senior captain and defender.

There I was, an offensive freshman playing defense on the game's biggest stage.

Petro was right.

CONFIDENCE ON DEMAND

Jay Williams had one of the all-time great college basketball careers at Duke. He was both the ACC Rookie of the Year and National Freshman of the Year. His sophomore year, he led Duke to win the NCAA Championship. In his junior year, he was awarded the Naismith and Wooden Award as college basketball's Player of the Year. His number 22 was retired on Senior Night, and he graduated from Duke as the sixth all-time scorer, leading to his second overall selection by the Chicago Bulls in the 2002 NBA Draft.

You wouldn't think guys like that can doubt themselves, but of course they do.

Jay once told me about a bad game he had at Duke. It was rattling because when you're *that* talented, you're not used to playing bad. And he had the experience a lot of athletes have when you're playing poorly: you lose your confidence really fast. The game gets faster, you begin to make uncharacteristic mistakes, and you grow increasingly frustrated with yourself.

Duke's team captain, Shane Battier, cuffed Jay, brought him close, and said, "You know the fastest way back to building confidence, Jay?"

Desperate, Jay only wanted the answer. "Fucking tell me!" he shouted in their impromptu huddle.

"Go support your teammates. Pat them on the back when they do well. Pick them up when they miss a shot. Because when you pat someone on the back, it comes right back to you."

If you want to build your confidence, go build somebody else's.

If you want to feel good, go make your teammates feel good.

Don't wait for a pat on the back—go pat someone else's and it will come right back to yours.

TURN WEAKNESS INTO STRENGTH

Early skateboarding did not have good equipment or ramps. It was a physical sport—you needed a certain amount of strength to yank a board up and out of the ramp to get air for a trick.

As a skinny kid, the legendary Tony Hawk shouldn't have been able to do things the other skateboarders were doing.

"My disadvantage," Tony told me, "was that I was really small. I was just too small to get the inertia. I didn't have the bulk behind me to get in the air like other skaters."

It seemed like a disadvantage up until the very moment that it drove him to innovate.

"I had to create my own way of getting in the air," he said. To get in the air, Tony began *ollieing* as he rode up a ramp. "I've been credited with being the first one to ollie into my aerials. It wasn't like I was trying to create a movement. I did it because I was desperate. I wanted to figure out how to get in the air. And I couldn't do it in the traditional way the bigger, older guys did it."

Tony changed skateboarding forever . . . out of desperation. Out of a weakness. A *perceived* disadvantage.

It's easy to sit back and make excuses for not being taller, faster, or stronger. For not being able to go to a better school or live in a certain place. And yes, this is unfortunate. It'd be ideal if things were always more fair, easier, and simpler. But what would the world be without adversity and difficulty? How many innovations would we be deprived of? How many breakthroughs would have never happened? How many better ways of doing things would have never been discovered?

You can turn your *perceived* weaknesses into strengths. You can transform your *perceived* disadvantages into game-changing innovations. You can use effort and tenacity to get in the air.

WHAT OTHER PEOPLE THINK

During Game 2 of the 2000 NBA Finals, Kobe Bryant sprained his ankle. He missed Game 3 and then played the rest of the series. And Kobe learned his lesson. "That was my worst sprain, but it certainly wasn't my first," he said. "I realized at that point I needed to be proactive about strengthening my ankles."

So he took up tap dancing.

He said, "After researching the matter, it became apparent that tap dancing was going to be the best way to build up my ankle strength while simultaneously improving my foot speed and rhythm."

What was the downside? His teammates would make fun of him? Fans might heckle him? He'd gladly trade that many times over if it meant no more ankle sprains—or better, a longer career. He'd gladly trade those condescending looks and jeers for a better crossover shake to fadeaway in the 2001 NBA Finals.

In 2014, I tore my lower rectus abdominis and left adductor. I had to undergo sports hernia surgery. My core was taking on too much strain from the hundreds of shots that were stacking up day after day. So, I decided to take barre class. I was the only guy in the room doing ballet squats—up an inch, down an inch. Deep lunges, high planks, and clamshells not only helped me repair my injury but improved my strength and agility. At twenty-nine, I was in better shape than when I was twenty-four.

Being afraid of looking silly or stupid is one of the biggest impediments for an athlete. When it comes to your game, you can't care about what other people think. You do what you need to do to get better, to learn something new, to grow a little stronger.

QUIET THE VOICES

Rafael Nadal says the toughest opponent in professional sports is one's internal dialogue.

"What I battle hardest to do in a tennis match," he writes in his memoir *Rafa*, "is to quiet the voices in my head. To shut everything out of my mind but the contest itself and concentrate every atom of my being on the point I am playing."

One of his weapons in this battle?

Ordering his environment. Before every match, he takes off his white warm-up jacket, places his tournament ID card on his bench facing up, sits, takes a sip from a bottle of water, takes another sip from a second bottle, then places the two bottles at his feet in front of his chair a little to the left, one neatly behind the other, diagonally aimed at the court.

"Some call it superstition," he writes, "but it's not. If it were superstition, why would I keep doing the same thing over and over whether I win or lose? It's a way of placing myself in a match, ordering my surroundings to match the order I seek in my head."

This is why basketball players have a free throw routine. This is why football kickers have a pre-kick ritual. This is why I would tear three pieces of athletic tape, pull out a black Sharpie, write my game intentions on them, and stick them to my locker before every game. It was part of ordering my surroundings before the game.

When you're feeling overwhelmed, when your internal dialogue is giving you trouble—try it: match the external to the internal state you seek.

FUNDAMENTALS

S hortly after training camp with the 1992 U.S. Olympic men's basketball team, Michael Jordan and Scottie Pippen were reflecting on what they had learned.

"Just imagine," Pippen said to Jordan, "how good Clyde Drexler would be if he worked on fundamentals."

Jordan's biographer writes, "Jordan had been surprised to learn how lazy many of his Olympic teammates were about practice, how they were deceiving themselves about what the game required."

Legendary basketball coach Morgan Wootten was the first high school coach to be inducted into the Naismith Memorial Basketball Hall of Fame. He would instruct us to stand in the paint under the hoop and make ten consecutive shots, using a complete follow-through, without hitting the rim. And when you did, you could take one step back and do it again. When you made ten straight there, you could take another step back. And so on.

I took that drill over to lacrosse. People would watch me practice from three yards away from the net and I knew what they were thinking—"*What's this fucking guy doing? Anyone can score from there.*" I was working on my fundamentals in the paint. And I didn't care what other people thought.

To pull off any impressive play, you first have to lay the foundation. To shoot behind the back, you first must become excellent at shooting overhand. To deceive a defender with a split dodge, you first must have terrific footwork. To throw a pass on a dime while rolling out to your left, you first must be automatic at throwing a pass on a dime while standing still.

You can become great on talent alone. But you can't become the champion you're capable of without working on the fundamentals.

Don't deceive yourself about what the game requires.

Be about practice.

WHAT'S YOUR ANCHOR?

The key to success for Dwayne "The Rock" Johnson was finding his anchor.

For Dwayne, this meant getting up at four o'clock in the morning, every day, before anybody else, and grounding his thought process in "No one will outwork me . . . no one."

Like a powerful anchor with two barbed flukes on either end, one is his discipline and the other, his belief.

WHAT DO YOU WANT TO DO WITH THIS?

In high school, Chris Bosh lived in the gym. Most of his memories lived there, working on his game. But there's one day that he'll never forget.

Bosh was working on his post moves when his coach caught him by surprise with a question he'd never been asked before:

"What do you want to do with this, Chris?"

Bosh was confused. *What do I want to do with this?*

Bosh was a hard worker—so he thought maybe his coach meant, *What do you want all this time and effort to accomplish?*

"I want to win a state championship," Bosh said. "And I want to get a college scholarship."

That's not what Coach had in mind. "He was thinking much bigger," Bosh said. "He was thinking beyond the game . . . He wanted me to think bigger, too."

What did you want to do with your life? Who did you want to be? Where could your talents take you, and where could you go if you put everything you had into driving toward your goals?

The weight of Coach's questions hit Bosh hard, causing him to reflect deeply on his purpose and potential. As he stood there, surrounded by the echoes of bouncing basketballs and the whispers of teammates, Bosh began to comprehend that sports are not merely a game—they are a platform for personal growth, a gateway to uncharted horizons, an agent of positive, widespread change.

"No matter what kind of talent you've been blessed with," Bosh writes in *Letters to a Young Athlete*, "you still have to answer the same question: What do you want to do with this? Where are you going, and how can you use what you've been given to get there?"

That is the question. Your actions, from here on out, are the answer.

*My life can be divided into two
parts: before turning pro and after.*

—STEVEN PRESSFIELD

You played for the love of the game. You enjoyed the freedom of being an amateur. You worked hard and cultivated range. You stuck with it. And then, you turned pro. Now you go all in. You have to *profess* yourself to your calling. You have to invest more of your time, more of your resources. To get an edge, you have to do things your competition isn't willing to do. You have to be comfortable with others not understanding why you do what you do as much as you do it. You have to say no to cool opportunities, stay in when everyone else is going out, and get up early when everyone else is sleeping in. You might have to change the way you prepare for and recover from a game. You have to put in more time and make more sacrifices than you ever have. It's not for everyone, but this is the reality. This is what it takes to be great. This is what it takes to be a professional . . .

GO ALL IN

In the 2008 Major League Lacrosse College Draft, I was selected first overall by the Boston Cannons. My rookie wage was $6,000. I was a college graduate from an elite university. I was considered the best player in the country. And my reward, my dream coming true, meant moving back home to live with my parents—not what you're used to seeing out of a professional athlete. I was making poverty-level wages . . . and had to get a day job just to afford food, let alone medical treatment and car insurance and gas and a gym membership and books and the rest.

But that's showbiz, baby. I took what I could get.

Which was far closer to the norm for basically every other domain in life. When a painter goes from amateur to professional, it's not usually to a sold-out gallery showing of six-figure paintings. A pro golfer or tennis player has to grind to make the tournament's cut, only to be in contention for prize money, while paying for their own entry or locker room fee, airfare, and hotel. A writer's life won't change with their first book deal—usually without an advance. Only in modern team sports leagues like the NBA or the NFL is getting drafted glamorous . . . and even then for only *some* of the picks.

In any case, there were still more indignities ahead.

Several months after I finished my rookie season, we hit a recession and even that day job went away.

It was another crossroads moment.

I could tap into my network and get some other corporate job. I could continue being an amateur—dabbling, finding pockets of time wherever I could to work on my game.

Or I could bet on myself. I could attempt what few players had attempted before.

I could go all in.

And that's what I did. I left my hometown to see how far I could take the sport of lacrosse. It was then—not when I was drafted—that I turned pro.

Turning pro isn't about getting drafted. It's not about "making it" to the league. It doesn't happen when you sign a rookie contract.

Turning pro is about the decisions *you* make. It's about making your craft your top and sole priority. It happens when you make the mindset shift—when you decide to go all in.

Are you ready to do that? Are you ready to turn pro?

YOU STILL CAN'T MISS A DAY

Even after you've made it to the pros . . . you still can't miss a day.

When you're the best player on the team . . . one hundred shots.

When you're the best player in the state . . . one hundred shots.

When you're the best player in the country . . . one hundred shots.

When you're the best player in the world . . . one hundred shots.

When you're named league MVP . . . one hundred shots.

When you win a championship . . . one hundred shots.

Book gets published—the next day . . . you write two hundred words.

Win a Grammy—the next day . . . you practice for two hours.

Close your round of financing—the next day . . . back to work.

Get married—the next day . . . accompany your partner as if it was the first date.

The professional knows that the work doesn't stop with success. They know that success is a by-product of the work. So they keep doing the work.

They don't miss a day.

INSANE ABOUT YOUR CRAFT

Wayne Gretzky was two years old when he learned to skate on ice behind his parents' home in Ontario, Canada. From that moment on, "The Great One" ate, drank, lived, and breathed hockey. Wanting to practice whenever and wherever he could, Gretzky never left home without his hockey stick. Although he was undersized his entire career, this unmatched dedication to the game and constant honing of his skills would lead him to four NHL Stanley Cups, a record nine MVP awards, as well as records for most career goals, assists, points, and hat tricks in a career.

He was insane. Insane about his craft.

When I was growing up, almost daily my mother would stand in the doorway of our home, one foot propping the screen door open, and yell, "Paul—dinner is on the table! Come inside!" Her pleas were drowned out by my focus on the next shot. I couldn't finish my practice without hitting ten corners in a row. Every day. That's when I knew it would be okay to go inside. It didn't matter if I was hungry, if I had homework, or if it was starting to pour.

It wasn't that I didn't feel hungry—I did. It wasn't that I would forgo doing my homework, either. There was a commitment to finishing the practice. There was an ability to push beyond thresholds of necessity because of how insane I was about my craft.

Like Gretzky, I would carry my stick with me inside after practice. I would prop it up in my bedroom before I went to sleep. It was the last thing I touched at night, and the first thing I picked up in the morning. It became a part of me.

Few understand this commitment. The world might try to slow you down. To temper your excessive effort. Even other athletes don't get it. They've asked me: *Why lacrosse? Why not a more popular sport that pays better?*

But it made perfect sense to me: This kind of singular focus is what would make me a better player. It was just who I was, what my daemon demanded.

Jim Carrey—one of the most versatile and iconic actors, known for his comedic performances, dynamic facial expressions, and memorable roles in film—said, "I have an insane belief in my own ability to manifest things." After years of fruitless auditions, Carrey drove up Mulholland Drive in Los Angeles, parked his car, sat outside, and overlooked Hollywood. He began to visualize his favorite studio executives and directors showing interest in him, as well as major opportunities coming his way. Carrey then wrote himself a check for $10 million, noting "acting services rendered," and dated it November 24, 1995—three years from the time he wrote it.

Just before Thanksgiving in 1995, Carrey agreed to a $10 million deal to star in the film *Dumb and Dumber*.

From here on out, you must have this level of focus and effort. You have to be an assassin with a relentless pursuit of becoming the best. You have to bring your stick everywhere. And you have to be insane enough to write yourself a $10 million check.

AIM TO BE THE ONLY

Before he was Jimi Hendrix, he went by Jimmy James.

In the 1960s, Jimmy James was a roadie and driver for the musician Little Richard.

Johnny Echols, a musician who toured with Little Richard, said James was decent at the guitar, but mainly, "he was the gofer."

Then in 1967, there was an invention called the Vox Wah-Wah pedal. Vox sent pedals to both Echols and Little Richard. Vox's pitch was, "This pedal will make your guitar sound like a trombone." Most musicians dismissed the pedal because, as Echols put it, "If I wanted the sound of the trombone, I would play the trombone, so I put the damn thing in the closet."

But Jimmy James started experimenting with the pedal.

And a year later, Echols got a phone call. "There's this incredible guitar player named Jimi Hendrix playing at The Whiskey tonight," Echols was told. "He sounds unlike any guitar player you've ever heard—you have to go see him."

The Whiskey wasn't far from where Echols was living at the time. "I went to The Whiskey expecting to see somebody that we didn't know," he said. But it was Jimmy James . . . playing the guitar with the Wah-Wah pedal.

"In the space of a little over a year," Echols said, "he goes from being just a so-so guitar player to being God basically. Without that [Wah-Wah pedal], there would have been no Jimi Hendrix. That's what made him sound different. And that's what made everybody look. Because he didn't sound like every other guitar player. He sounded different."

Billionaire entrepreneur Peter Thiel likes to say that *competition is for losers*. Whether you're an entrepreneur, a writer, or a guitar player, Thiel said, "You want to aim for monopoly. . . . You want to be one of a kind. You don't want to be the fourth online pet food company, the tenth thin film solar panel company, or the hundredth restaurant in Palo Alto."

You don't want to be the millionth so-so guitar player. You want to aim to sound unlike any other guitar player.

You want to be what only you can be . . . *you.*

Perhaps there's a Wah-Wah pedal out there that you or your teammates or colleagues haven't tried yet. In basketball, dribbling through your legs and behind your back was once considered showboating. Today, the skill is used to gain an advantage through agility and deception. Same was the case for a behind-the-back pass in lacrosse during the '80s and '90s. Today, we see it during every possession.

Is there a different way you can play the game?

I n 1984, while studying at the University of Texas at Austin, Michael Dell started a computer company called PC's Limited from his dorm room.

The company initially sold upgraded IBM-compatible PCs directly to customers, cutting out the middleman and offering lower prices. Dell's business model gained popularity, and the company quickly grew. In 1988, the company was renamed Dell Computer Corporation, and eventually, it became known as Dell Technologies, the world's largest IT infrastructure company.

In the appendix of his book *Play Nice but Win*, Dell shares a collection of principles, traits, and lessons that shaped his success. Among these valuable insights is the phrase "Be pleased but never satisfied," which Dell explains:

> This means improving continuously—the Japanese call it *kaizen*. It means being in a race with no finish line. Celebrate and appreciate achievements, but always look ahead to the next big goal or opportunity.

What I love about this phrase is how it creates room for a sense of accomplishment on the ambitious path of continuous improvement.

Those of us with the never-enough mentality, who get back to work the day after winning a championship, who are constantly striving to grow, learn, and advance often forget to stop for a moment to acknowledge and appreciate the fulfillment derived from one's achievements. This sense of fulfillment can be a vital fuel for sustained progress in the long run.

Be pleased but never satisfied. On the flip side, if you are always solely fixated on what is yet to be achieved, you are perpetually dissatisfied. If you are perpetually dissatisfied, you will burn out before you realize your full potential.

GO DEEP

K evin Plank cofounded Under Armour with Kip Fulks. Together, they have generated over $50 billion in sales. In college, Fulks was a walk-on who became a scholarship lacrosse player at perennial power University of Maryland (and then played professionally for ten years). Today, he owns and operates Big Truck Farms and Brewery, where he has learned from scratch how to craft beer.

The thread running through his outsize successes, Fulks said, is that he goes all in.

Also an avid bow hunter, Fulks analogizes his success to bow hunting. If you're thinking about anything but hitting the monster bull at fifty yards, you don't hit the monster bull.

"Go deep," he said. "Don't do anything else—that's my point. If I would have stopped along the way and said, 'Oh I want to be a stockbroker,' or, 'I want to learn how to kite surf'—no I don't have fucking time for any of that shit. I had to learn how to brew and grow hops. So for the last seven years, that's all I've been doing. . . . If you're struggling in life, I ask you if you have consistency."

Want to talk about consistency? One of basketball's best pure shooters ever, JJ Reddick, said that his off-seasons were harder than the season. From June to October, six days a week, with two to three workouts a day, and Saturdays for rest and recovery, Reddick would then shoot 342 shots on Sundays. When asked why 342, he said, "It's very simple, man. There are seven spots on the floor. Twenty spot twos . . . twenty spot threes . . . three dribbles going right, three dribbles going left . . . plus twenty free throws. That's 342."

Turning pro, being consistent, being insane about your craft—requires sacrifice. There's no more sampling and dabbling. Not with stocks, not with kites, not with your free time, nothing. You don't have time for any of that shit anymore.

REDUCE TO PRODUCE PERFECTION

In a video of Jay-Z and Rick Rubin in the recording studio working on the song "99 Problems," Rubin suggests the idea to cut the beat and open the song a cappella.

This approach—reducing down, cutting away—is characteristic of Rubin. On the very first album Rubin produced, the credit he took was "reduced by Rick Rubin," instead of "produced by Rick Rubin."

"I like to get to the essential," Rubin said. "Often in the studio, when you try to build upon things, when you add layers to try to make it sound bigger—often, the more things you add, the smaller it gets."

This kind of reduction is also characteristic of getting better. Think of the smooth stroke of a Michael Phelps versus the kicking and flailing of a kid learning to swim. The fluid swing of an Aaron Judge versus the uncontrolled swing of a Little Leaguer. The graceful spin through the air of an Olympic gymnast versus the wild and jerky rotation of a beginner.

When I first learned how to cradle, I incorporated it into every one of my moves—before a dodge, pass, and shot. In college, though, my coach showed me how this was a "wasted motion." I had developed a handle for my stick with a quick release that no longer required me to cradle ahead of every dodge, pass, and shot.

As we get better at something, we reduce down to the essential motions and movements.

That's why it's called *honing* your skills. It's a stripping away of unnecessary motions to achieve efficiency and precision. The smooth stroke of Phelps's swimming reflects countless hours spent perfecting his technique, eliminating any unnecessary resistance in the water. Similarly, Aaron Judge's fluid swing in baseball stems from tireless training, enabling him to make precise contact with the ball. Olympic gymnasts demonstrate astonishing control and elegance in their aerial maneuvers, having refined their movements to achieve maximum grace and skill.

It is not just in sports. The process of improving anything is a process of refinement. For the process of writing a book, I learned, is about continuously cutting and refining. All the way through recording the audiobook, we were finding things to cut, ways to make this book more concise.

"Perfection is achieved," Antoine de Saint-Exupéry famously wrote, "not when there is nothing more to add, but when there is nothing left to take away."

HOW MANY THINGS HAVE YOU SAID NO TO?

In a practice similar to the process of improving, those who are world-class at what they do whittle their to-do lists down to the essential.

Jony Ive has more than five thousand patents, twice as many as Thomas Edison. Here are just some of the products he's designed:

iPhone
AirPods
Apple Watch
iPad
MacBook Air
iPod
iPod Mini
iMac

How did he do it?

Focus. And not the kind of focus meaning that you work on a task without getting distracted.

"What focus means," Ive says, "is saying no to something that you—with every bone in your body—think is a phenomenal idea, and you wake up thinking about it, but you say no to it because you're focusing on something else."

It's about sacrifice. When Ive first started working at Apple, Steve Jobs told him, "Jony, you have to understand: there are measures of focus, and one of them is how often you say no."

Routinely, Jobs would ask, "Jony, how many things have you said no to today?"

This kind of focus, Ive admits, "takes so much effort . . . But all of the good things we've done have required that sort of focus."

This is what being a pro requires. This is what it means to be insane about your craft. It's saying no to those happy hour drinks to say yes to an hour of extra shooting. Saying no to the weekend away to say yes to a long weekend of two-a-days. Saying no to staying up late to play video games to say yes to waking up early to go to the gym.

During many moments of my journey, I've said no to pleasure so that I can say yes to commitment. I said no to the NFL to say yes to lacrosse. In 2022, after one of my best seasons as a pro, I said no to playing to say yes to building the PLL. Right now, I'm saying no to whatever I could do on my phone, whatever meeting I could be attending, whatever fun thing I could go do, to write this sentence, just as you are saying no to those things to focus and read it.

If you're struggling, I ask you, how many things have you said no to?

THESE ARE YOUR FIVE CHOICES

Arguably the greatest coach in college football history, Nick Saban, the University of Alabama's head coach, put it plain and simple.

In life, he said, we have five choices: to be bad, average, good, excellent, or elite. To reach excellence or elite status, one must exhibit special intensity, focus, commitment, drive, and passion—maintaining a high standard consistently.

"You have to have special intensity," said Saban. "You have to have special focus. You have to have a special commitment and drive and passion to do things at a high level. [You have to have] a high standard all the time."

Highly acclaimed filmmaker and Academy Award winner Martin Scorsese is known for his masterful storytelling prowess and profound commitment to his craft. Famously, he said, "Films are not films to me. They're life."

In other words, regardless of our God-given abilities, achieving excellence requires a life commitment.

It's up to you.

Becoming a champion is a choice, a mindset, a relentless drive to continuously improve and strive for greatness. Reaching the highest levels of success requires going beyond what is expected or considered good, and consistently challenging oneself to reach new heights.

SEIZE THE SHORT WINDOW

After the Denver Nuggets won the 2023 NBA Finals, Finals MVP Nikola Jokic said he was excited to get home to Sombor, Serbia, to see his horses.

Growing up, Jokic said a few years earlier, "I had two older brothers who played basketball. I fell in love with basketball because of them. We would always play together. But then at some point in my life I started to go into horse racing. I just fell in love with horses and their beauty and elegance. It was like a hobby for me. I didn't get serious with it. And I wasn't taking basketball serious, either. I was in between both."

Jokic came to a crossroads. He had to make the decision we've been talking about: What would he go pro in? What would he make his main thing? What craft would he become insane about?

"He started growing, both in height and in size, and he started to become aware that he could be a basketball player," Jokic's dad said. But Jokic was leaning toward horses. "He would say, 'Dad, I want to become a horseman.' And I used to tell him: 'Son, become a basketball player first, and you'll become a great horseman later.'"

Sports, for the most part, are ageist. They are a young person's game. The older we get, the more our bodies wear and tear, and the less athletic we become.

There is a short window in which you can take your sport to the elite level. Become insane about your craft first, and follow your passions—become a great horseman or guitar player or entrepreneur or investor—later.

YOU CAN'T REALLY DO TWO THINGS AT ONCE

t was 2019, and I was struggling.

My brother, Mike, and I had just launched the Premier Lacrosse League and I was playing for one of our six teams—Atlas Lacrosse Club. I was taking on the most rigorous and complex schedule of my career.

To be the best on the field, I knew that my commitment to performance needed to outpunch that of my competitors. To be the best business owner, the same rules applied.

Every day I would wake up at 7:00 a.m. and head to the gym for an hour to train, then head to the field to shoot. Like clockwork, two and a half hours of getting it in, followed by a quick shower and over to the office to build the PLL until ten or eleven o'clock at night.

Day in, day out. Rinse and repeat.

I had a below-average first season in the PLL.

Director, producer, writer, actor, boxing enthusiast, and friend Peter Berg would take me for a workout once a month at his Santa Monica gym, Churchill Boxing. After a big workout that ended with his patented ab circuit to no end—only muscle failure—we began to discuss my dual approach to playing and building the PLL.

Pete told me, "You actually can't do two things at once *really* well. You can build the PLL well for a few hours, then train well for a few hours . . . but after each day, you're leaving something on the table."

MIT Sloane's Neurological Science Department demonstrated that the human brain is incapable of focusing on two things at once. Multitasking is a myth. Walking and chewing gum isn't in the same stratosphere as having the desire to become a champion in sport *and* in business.

I eventually had to choose.

M y head coach in our first season of the PLL was the mindful and meditative John Paul.

After our third game, JP pulled me aside. He saw my pregame preparation and asked, "Have you thought about ratcheting it down a little bit? You're a skill player—have you explored being a little calmer before games?"

It had never occurred to me. I grew up playing contact sports with my brother, Mike. We loved the up-tempo preparation. I often had System of a Down or Rage Against the Machine in my headphones ahead of a practice, workout, or game. I flourished in the intensity of the moment. I played at my best angry, pissed off, intense—ready for contact.

But I thought I'd give it a shot. I listened to classic jazz, slower-paced music . . . and I went out to the game and registered zero goals and zero assists. I felt lethargic.

I learned from that experience.

In the locker room, you can find me hanging out with the defenders. Where the intensity brews. Those are my guys. That's my kind of energy. Big Mike energy.

For most of my years as a captain, I would try to convince everyone to match my intensity. And if they didn't turn up like I was before games, I would feel frustrated and deflated. The way I saw it, they weren't ready to go.

Only until recently I learned a simple truth—everyone's different.

Two years after JP, I suited up with one of the greatest players in the world—Lyle Thompson. Before games, he's quiet and calm. He's in the corner meditating. He doesn't scream, jump, or headbutt his teammates. Kyle Harrison was similar—kept it light and focused. Gary Gait, the man I think was the greatest to ever play the game, looked rather pedestrian in the locker room. These guys, all profound players in their own right, preferred to protect their energy in the locker room.

To perform at his best, Tom Brady needed to create a heightened sense of emotion before a game. He achieved this through anger. When Brady was angry, it would elevate his focus and awareness. He said, "Anger is good because it was motivating." The more Brady could create an enemy out of his opponent, the easier it would be for him to get into a mindset of peak performance.

There is no right or wrong way to prepare for a game. You gotta find your way. And you gotta leave everyone else to theirs.

LOVE A LITTLE STRUGGLE

Chris Bosh said something he learned from Kobe Bryant was that "you gotta love the parts that aren't fun, you gotta love a little struggle."

Playing in the NBA is fun. Practicing, lifting, conditioning, and sacrificing enough to make it to—and *in*—the NBA is a struggle.

Publishing a book is fun. Writing, researching, contemplating, and rewriting is a struggle.

Acing a client presentation is fun. Ideating, preparing, producing, and rehearsing the pitch is a struggle.

Bosh said he has this thing he says to himself anytime he's struggling:

"I always like to think, 'How many people would quit right now?' That's the first thing I think about. Then I keep going."

CONFRONT THE BRUTAL REALITY

When Hugh Jackman set out to be an actor, he made a contract with himself: "Give it seven days a week for five years."

"When I started at drama school," he explained, "I was the dunce of the class. It just wasn't coming right to me. . . . Everyone seemed more likely to succeed, everyone seemed more natural at it." He confronted the reality that if he were to succeed, it would require that he work seven days a week for five years, at least.

The highly decorated United States Navy admiral, James Stockdale, survived nearly eight years in a Vietnam prison camp. For nearly eight years, Admiral Stockdale was tortured and subjected to unimaginable loneliness and terror.

When later asked who struggled the most in those prison camps, Stockdale said, paradoxically, that it was the optimists who got crushed. The ones who deceived themselves, who lied to themselves, who set unrealistic expectations for their release were emotionally devastated and mentally broken by having their hopes repeatedly dashed.

In order to endure dark circumstances, Stockdale said, "You must never confuse faith that you will prevail in the end—which you can never afford to lose—with the discipline to confront the most brutal facts of your current reality, whatever they might be."

This balance of believing you will prevail while also accepting your brutal reality has become known as the Stockdale Paradox—embraced far beyond the POW context.

When Jackman set out to be an actor, he set out with this special blend of realistic optimism. While he maintained the belief that he could make it, he confronted the brutal fact that it might take half a decade of working and training seven days a week.

It's the athlete confronting the reality of their injury, then doing what it takes to come back stronger. It's the entrepreneur confronting the reality that their initial idea isn't working, then pivoting and finding success in a different way.

Confront the brutal reality—right now. Of your current abilities. Of your injury. Of your team's prospects. Of your height. Of the odds of making it into the big leagues. Of the situation you got yourself into. Don't give in to wishful thinking. Don't lie to yourself. Accept what it is, fully, completely, honestly.

And then?

Get to work doing something about it. Prevail in the end, somehow, someway.

A LESSON

At twenty-eight years old, Tyson Fury was an undefeated World Heavy-weight Champion. He was also about to kill himself—driving his sports car at 160 miles per hour toward a bridge. He might have succeeded too, he said, until a voice came inside his head to remind him of his family, his kids, and the feeling that if he gave up it would be an act of weakness.

Weakness is the antithesis of boxing.

Tyson competed against giants in one of the toughest, most grueling sports in the world. He recalls how difficult it was to communicate his struggles and unhappiness among the machismo of boxing.

"I used to wake up every day and feel terrible."

On that fateful night, Tyson would eventually pull the car over and call his dad to come pick him up. Shortly after, he would check himself in to counseling and begin to heal.

"I've had the opportunity to be shot down, and you never know what you've really gotten until it's gone."

Many in the boxing world thought Tyson's career was over. That a boxer in therapy was going to soften his edge in the ring.

By thirty-five, Tyson had won another five World Heavyweight Championship matches. He was more dominant than ever, stronger in the ring, but most importantly, outside of it.

TAKE CARE OF YOUR WHOLE SELF

On the way to her first professional tennis tournament in Oakland, California, Venus Williams got advice she never forgot.

Venus had been a dominant amateur tennis player, and her success was about to propel her into the national spotlight. Heading into this new phase of her life, Venus wrote, "My mother told me this: If I wanted to thrive in this sport—and in life—I needed to take care of my 'whole self.'"

To that point, training to be a great tennis player meant focusing on her physical training, physical preparation, and physical health.

But, her mother knew, the body is only half of it. "What my mom was telling me that day in Oakland was that . . . I also [needed to] tend to my mental health."

That's what Tyson Fury had to learn to do. It's what we all have to learn to do because our insanity and commitment to greatness at something must be balanced.

Venus sought out mental health professionals "to help me see more clearly—not to let my fears distort my reality—and to develop my ability to learn to stay in the moment."

Kobe Bryant described his reading habit as another version of a mindfulness practice, a way to "strengthen my ability to be present and not have a wandering mind."

As you transition from amateur to professional, you must begin to think holistically. To look after your psychological well-being. To learn how to handle, as Venus wrote, "the inevitable psychological issues that bubble up for all of us."

As a professional, you must begin to take care of your whole self.

SLEEP IS A DISCIPLINE

Soldiers talk about "sleep discipline"—the practice, *the work*, of maintaining a structured and regulated sleep routine. When a military operation requires soldiers to work around the clock, for instance, a crucial component of their sleep discipline is the "tactical nap." Whenever there is a twenty-minute window, soldiers take a tactical nap, banking the energy needed to carry out the mission.

By prioritizing sleep discipline, military personnel mitigate the risks associated with sleep deprivation and optimize their performance in high-stress and demanding environments.

It's not just in the military. High performers, especially those who sustain their high performance over a long period of time, have sleep discipline.

There was a stretch in 2021 in which a thirty-seven-year-old LeBron James played back-to-back road games in the Midwest, made a stop in Phoenix to watch his son play, and then went out and had a triple-double against the Orlando Magic on a Sunday night. LeBron was asked how he does it, where he gets all his energy. "Sleep," he said. Even within that busy stretch, he prioritized sleep. "I slept last night from 12 to 8. I got up, ate breakfast, and then I went back to sleep from 8:30 to 12:30."

LeBron, teammates joke, is always either playing basketball or sleeping.

JUST WHEN YOU THOUGHT IT WAS OVER

After finishing eleventh in the all-around at the 2018 U.S. National Gymnastics Championships, Jordan Chiles was ready to check out of the sport.

"I guess this sport is coming to an end for me," Chiles said. "Things just aren't working out for me at all whatsoever." So she made up her mind to quit gymnastics after high school and transition to college as a student only. "But then I had a talk with Simone."

Simone Biles, the world's greatest gymnast, told Chiles she should move to Texas and train with her. Two days after graduating from high school, Chiles moved to Texas. She began training with Biles every day, and it quickly began to show. At her first event, four weeks after moving to Texas, a former Olympian in attendance would recall "being shocked at how good she looked."

At the 2019 U.S. National Championships, Chiles finished sixth in the all-around—good enough to earn a spot on the national team. After competition was canceled for the 2020 season due to COVID-19, Chiles placed first in the all-around at the first major competition of 2021. A few months later, she placed second in the all-around at the U.S. Classic behind . . . Simone Biles.

As a result, she was selected to compete at the Olympic Trials, where she placed third. Just three years after almost quitting the sport, Chiles was named to the U.S. Olympic team.

You can rise to your potential. Or you can fall to the level of the mean. You can find your Simone Biles. Or you can repeatedly put yourself in situations where you're the best player.

Spend your time with those who will push and pull you up to their level of greatness.

YOUR FIRST DATE

The first date is always exciting, just like the first practice of the season is. We train every day to improve our conditioning, our skill, and our game intelligence. We eat properly, stay hydrated, and sleep for eight hours so we can perform our best on game days.

Yet often with romance, once things settle into a routine, we don't always show up like we did at the beginning, when everything felt fresh and new. We can become complacent.

Think of it like this: What if we decided to show up to practice half-focused, with average output? What if you became complacent on the field? How would that reflect on you? On your coaches? On your teammates?

Champions don't approach practice with their shoulders slouched, distracted, wishing they were doing something else. They don't go through the motions.

What if we approached our romances with the same effort that we bring to practice?

CONSTANTLY EXPOSE YOURSELF TO GREATNESS

W hen he was coming up as a writer, the author and journalist Rex Murphy would write out his favorite poems and passages.

He was asked, *What's that done for you?*

"There's an energy attached to poetry and great prose," Murphy said. "And when you bring it into your mind, into your living sensibility, by some weird osmosis, it lifts your style or the attempts of your mind."

When you read great writing, when you write down a great line or paragraph, Murphy continued, "somehow or another, it contaminates you in a rich way. You get something from it—from this osmotic imitation."

In my phone I have an album of photos containing the most iconic moments in sports. It's called "The Way of the Champion." Michael Jordan hugging the trophy after winning the 1991 NBA Finals. Wilt Chamberlain in the locker room after scoring 100 points. Usain Bolt smiling as he crosses the finish line in first at the Olympics. Brandi Chastain after her winning penalty kick in the 1999 Women's World Cup. Lionel Messi on the shoulders of his teammate Sergio Agüero, hoisting his first World Cup. Muhammad Ali standing over Sonny Liston. Kerri Strug being carried to the podium after she tore two ligaments in her ankle *and then* clinched the first-ever team gold medal for the U.S. women's gymnastics team. Willie Mays making one of the most miraculous catches in baseball history, which would help the Giants win the World Series. Arnold Schwarzenegger, Bill Belichick, Tom Brady, Tiger Woods, Serena Williams, Secretariat—the list goes on.

Before a big game, a big meeting, a big day—I flip through this album. I expose myself to and meditate on greatness. I let it contaminate me. And through osmosis, I become a little bit more like them.

INSPIRATION VERSUS ACHIEVEMENT

A fter winning his fifth Grammy and Album of the Year, Jon Batiste was onstage being recognized as the best of the best. Yet he said this:

> There is no best musician, best artist, best dancer, best actor. The creative arts are subjective, and they reach people at a point in their lives when they need it most.

During challenging times, sport can serve as a resilient source of inspiration, foster unity, and instill a sense of purpose in us. It can provide a collective escape that transcends individual struggles—offering hope and strength when we need it most.

FACE THE LOSSES

n 2002, Bill Belichick made his first Super Bowl appearance as a head coach. His New England Patriots were going up against the heavily favored St. Louis Rams—a team they lost to in the regular season. Preparation for the rematch began with Belichick telling his team that *he* had a poor coaching performance in the first game against the Rams.

"I'm not going to screw up again," he promised them.

So Belichick went and "looked endlessly at the film of that game," his biographer David Halberstam writes. He watched that regular season loss, start to finish, over and over and over. What was he looking for? He didn't exactly know. But he began to see something interesting. By his count, the Patriots had sent five or more defensive players after the Rams' quarterback forty-two times. They never sacked him.

In that first matchup, the legendary quarterback Kurt Warner threw for 401 yards and three touchdowns. Their three top receivers combined for 289 yards and two touchdowns.

In the Super Bowl, Belichick adjusted. Instead of sending defensive players after the quarterback, he put two, and sometimes three, defenders on the Rams' receivers. The result? Those same three Rams' receivers combined for just 159 yards and zero touchdowns.

The Patriots won Super Bowl XXXVI, 20-17.

One NFL analyst, after watching eight hours of film on the game, called it "the best coaching job I've ever seen."

The lesson—making strategic adjustments based on lessons learned from prior performance—can be derived from Belichick's strategy in winning a Super Bowl and broadly applied. CEOs and project managers use what is known as a postmortem, which is simply a process of analyzing and evaluating a completed project, event, or situation to identify strengths, weaknesses, and areas for improvement.

The essence of the postmortem lies in the willingness to reflect on past experiences, objectively evaluate performance, and learn from mistakes or shortcomings.

This can be hard to do.

During the summer after the UConn women's basketball team lost to Notre Dame in the finals of the 2018 NCAA tournament, UConn star Katie Lou Samuelson bumped into Kobe Bryant.

"Have you watched the Notre Dame game?" Kobe asked.

"No," Samuelson said, "I don't want to watch that."

"I know you don't," Kobe said, "but you're going to play Notre Dame this year, right?"

Yeah.

"There's a chance you see them again in the final, right?"

Yeah.

"Well, you can't show up and play them without knowing why you lost the last one. You have to watch that game and study that game. You can't make the same mistakes over and over again just because you weren't brave enough to face it. You gotta deal with it. Face it. Learn from it."

As hard as it can be, you gotta face your losses and failures. You gotta study them and figure out why they happened. Only then can you learn from them, make adjustments, and improve.

WHAT TO SAY AFTER A BIG LOSS

Someone who knows that losing is just part of being one of the greats is Novak Djokovic. Right after losing to Carlos Alcaraz in the 2023 Wimbledon Final, Djokovic made his remarks. Four parts stood out to me.

His perspective: "Obviously you never like to lose matches like this but I guess when all the emotions are settled, I have to still be very grateful because I won many, many tight and close matches in the past."

His competitive fire: "I will be [proud of my achievements] tomorrow morning, probably. Today, not so much. Obviously, tough one to swallow, you know?"

His gratitude: "I've been blessed with so many incredible matches throughout my career. So this is just another one in the history books for me. I'm really, really grateful even though, of course, I did not win today."

His humility: "I lost to a better player. I have to congratulate him and move on—stronger, hopefully."

The thirty-six-year-old Djokovic was asked if this was the start of a rivalry with the twenty-year-old Alcaraz. "Ha, I hope so," he said. "For my sake. He's going to be on the tour for quite some time. I don't know how long I'll be around."

Perhaps the only undefeated player in sports came out on top again . . . Father Time.

THERE ARE NO LOSSES, ONLY LESSONS

When Major League Lacrosse took a break in action for the 2014 World Lacrosse Championships, I was playing the best ball of my career.

Midway through the tournament, I got a text from Denver Outlaws coach Tony Seaman—yes, the same Coach Seaman who once told me to shoot one hundred shots a day. This time, he told me how great we were playing, and that we could go down as the best USA team ever.

After an opening game 10-7 win against Team Canada, we coasted into the gold medal game for a rematch against them. Our confidence was so high that we packed goggles for a post-game locker room champagne celebration. We beat them earlier in the tournament. We beat them in the 2010 gold medal game. We weren't going to lose to Canada on U.S. soil.

To Canada's credit, they game-planned the hell out of us. They took the air out of the ball, they slowed the game down, and their goalie had his best game of the tournament. In the first half, we had just one goal on five shots. They took an 8-2 lead into the fourth quarter and held on to win 8-5. I had zero goals and zero assists.

Perhaps the greatest USA team ever assembled lost to Canada in front of a home crowd of twenty thousand fans and more watching on ESPN. It was at a time when lacrosse was getting more exposure and attention across social media, with better television distribution—and pending a win, I was even booked to do late-night TV.

But we lost. And I let my teammates—and country—down.

A week later, I returned to MLL action, and in a game to clinch a playoff berth, I broke my foot. It was a remarkably devastating few weeks. I went from being the best player in the world to having the worst game of my career to breaking my foot and staring down the barrel of a six-month recovery. I couldn't sleep. I was reliving every play in my head. The missed shots. The bad turnovers. I was depressed.

My brother convinced me to hire a sports psychologist. I was introduced to John Eliot, a PhD from Stanford who's worked with the San Antonio Spurs, San Francisco Giants, and Team USA Basketball, to name a few.

Once a week, John and I would talk for hours on end. Prior to meeting him, lacrosse was my identity. Full stop. And that was a dangerous place to be.

When things were great, I felt like I was on cloud nine. When I lost or riddled the stat sheet with mistakes, I couldn't move on. It was lacrosse—and nothing else mattered.

I had to evolve into a mindset where the game was no longer who I was—it was just something I did. I had to learn that losing to Canada in the gold medal game wasn't the biggest failure of my life. It was a really important life lesson. It helped me grow—personally and professionally. It also ignited a fire within me. One that made me holistically better.

I got back to my roots of playing the game for fun. I was more intellectual in my approach—enjoying every moment, feeling grateful to play, and reinvesting in relationships on and off the field.

Like any big loss, the lesson forced me to rework my routine and think critically about ways I could improve.

In 2014, I thought I was playing the best ball of my career. As it happened, I was wrong. In 2015, I registered the most points in my career, brought a championship back to New York for the first time in ten years, and was named the Championship Game MVP.

Then, four years later, with one second left in regulation of the 2018 World Lacrosse gold medal game, we scored to win, 9-8.

Against Canada.

THE GREATS LOSE . . . A LOT

Bill Belichick is one of the *losingest* coaches in NFL history. Most likely, he will become *the* losingest coach in NFL history. At the time of this writing, he is just fourteen losses away from breaking the record. He's also won the most Super Bowls of any NFL coach in history.

Tom Brady, John Elway, Drew Brees, Peyton Manning, and Dan Marino are all in the top twenty of quarterbacks who have thrown the most interceptions. Peyton's twenty-eight interceptions thrown as a rookie in 1998 are still the most in NFL history. He's also fourth all-time for the most passing attempts in NFL history.

Martin Brodeur is the goalie with the most losses in NHL history. He also holds the record for the most career wins, games started, and shutouts. Cy Young is the pitcher with the most losses in MLB history. He also holds the record for the most career wins, games started, innings pitched, and complete games. Mark Zuckerberg has watched Meta's market cap decline by some of the largest single-day drops in market history. He's also built a trillion-dollar market cap company. Metallica has multiple albums their fans think are duds. They've also won nine Grammys. Michael Jordan missed over nine thousand shots in his career, lost almost three hundred times, and missed twenty-six game-winning shots—all as a six-time NBA Champion and six-time Finals MVP.

This is both a philosophical point and simple math: To win a lot, you have to risk losing a lot. If you stick around, those losses are going to add up—that can't scare or scar you. Losing is a by-product of being good enough and not quitting.

MAKE IT WORK FOR YOU

In 2007, a month before the rapper 50 Cent was planning to release a single from his third album, *Curtis*, the single somehow leaked to the internet.

When 50 Cent's team at the record label Interscope learned of the leak, they saw a great reason to panic. But when 50 Cent himself learned of the leak, he saw a great opportunity. He told his team to settle down.

"We're going to make this work for us," he told them.

A student of the book *The 48 Laws of Power* by Robert Greene, 50 Cent turned to law 37: create compelling spectacles.

50 Cent strategically lost his cool. He was like Bill Belichick using a bad call as a chance to fight with the refs to motivate his players. He was like Michael Jordan using a minor slight from an opponent as fuel for the forthcoming game.

He threw his phone. He pulled a TV off the wall and smashed it. He yelled and screamed and aggressively pointed blame. Pictures and video of the damage were "leaked" and the story spread everywhere. The spectacle helped *Curtis* debut at number two on the Billboard 200 chart.

"Events in life are not negative or positive," Greene writes. "They are completely neutral. . . . Things merely happen to you. It is your mind that chooses to interpret them as negative or positive."

When you're injured . . . make it work for you. I broke my foot twice, tore my left and right rectus abdominals, had two herniated discs in my lower back, a tear in both my right and left labrum, and very little cartilage left in my right knee. I've used these misfortunes as a chance to strengthen opposite ends of my body, watch film to improve my lacrosse IQ, build better mindfulness practices into my day, change my diet, and work on my stick skills from a seated position.

When you don't make the playoffs . . . make it work for you. Get a jump on the offseason training program, as there's no greater motivation than finishing your season with a loss.

NBA MVP Giannis Antetokounmpo said "There is no failure in sports" during his postgame press conference following the Milwaukee Bucks Game 5 series-ending loss to the Miami Heat in the first round of the 2023 NBA Playoffs. "So [for the] fifty years, from 1971 to 2021, we (Milwaukee Bucks) did not win a championship, it was fifty years of failure?" he asked the reporter. "No, it was not," Giannis continued. "It was steps to it. And then we were able to win one. Hopefully we can win another one."

In the 1960s, IBM CEO Tom Watson Jr. called an employee into his office after his venture lost $10 million. The man assumed he was being fired. "Fired?" Watson said. "Hell, I spent $10 million educating you. I just want to be sure you learned the right lessons."

There's no good or bad. There's what happens and then what you do with it. Always find a way to make it work for you.

THE PENDULUM SWINGS

S ome of the best players have some of the worst games.

In the 2003 season opener, Tom Brady completed fourteen of twenty-eight passes for 123 yards and four interceptions in a 31-0 loss against the Bills. The following week, he completed thirty of forty-four passes for 255 yards and three touchdowns in a 31-10 win against the Eagles.

After Steph Curry was the unanimous 2015–16 NBA MVP, he went 4 for 14 on 3-point attempts in a Game 7 loss of that year's finals.

In 2022, trillion-dollar market cap company, Meta, had the largest single-day drop ($232 *billion*) in the history of the U.S. stock market. It topped the record set by Apple ($182 billion) a year and a half earlier.

Everything in life is on a pendulum. The better you are, the greater the velocity of your swings. When you swing high, you can be the best player in the world. But that upward swing can also supply the energy to whip back in the other direction. As it did for me in that gold medal game against Canada.

Things that go up must come down.

If you practice hard, desire to win at all costs, and then lose a game— and it's inevitable that you *will* lose—it's going to be incredibly painful.

If you lift a lot of weight and run sprints every day, you're putting loads of pressure on your joints. You're wagering improved strength, speed, and better performance at the risk of a higher injury rate and long-term wear and tear.

When you are at an extreme—when things are going well or unwell— remind yourself that the swing in the other direction is just a matter of time. That you can't have the swing up without the swing down. And you can't swing back up without experiencing the pain of the downswing. Just commit to the experience and trust that you'll come around.

TREAT THESE IMPOSTORS JUST THE SAME

B lake Mycoskie—the founder of TOMS Shoes, a company that popularized the one-for-one business model—journals every day.

He usually writes and reflects on the previous day or week. He tries to keep in mind that his future self may want to learn from the experiences of his past self. So when he's going through a challenging experience, he's found it helpful to go back to a previously challenging time and look at what he was writing then in his journal.

"Oftentimes," Blake explained, "I find that what felt really challenging in the moment wasn't so challenging in hindsight. Keeping that in mind helps me deal with challenging situations in real time." He references one of his favorite quotes—from the poem "If" by Rudyard Kipling:

> If you can meet with Triumph and Disaster / And treat those two impostors just the same.

"My journal has taught me that over and over again," Blake said. "Nothing's as good as it was when I was writing it down. And nothing's as challenging as it was when I was writing it down."

I have felt the same disorienting sense of loss from missing a shot in the second quarter of a regular-season game as I have scoring zero points and losing a World Championship game. Definitively, there is a difference between both results, but knowing that neither outcome is as challenging as it was when I was experiencing it has helped point me in the direction of better play and better sequels.

We will experience plenty of good and bad days throughout our lives. There will be challenging moments of disaster and bad luck, as well as wonderful strokes of triumph and good luck.

We must embrace the swings of life and meet it all the same.

THIS TOO SHALL PASS

As a student, Tom Hanks said, "I was a geek. I was horribly, painfully, terribly shy."

Tom found his calling in college, studying drama at Cal State. He was so in love with it that he would "just drive to a theater, buy myself a ticket, sit in the seat and read the program, and then get into the play completely."

In the late 1970s, Tom moved to New York City, where he first got into the movie business, taking a small part in a 1980 horror film called *He Knows You're Alone*. Shortly thereafter, his stature in the film industry rose.

For over forty years Tom has acted, directed, produced, and written major motion pictures, winning a total of fifty awards, including Academy Awards, Golden Globes, and Lifetime Achievements.

From *Philadelphia* to *Forrest Gump* to *Saving Private Ryan*, Tom has starred in some of my favorite films. I thought to myself, this guy must walk on water.

Of course, that's not true.

Even Tom Hanks has struggled in his career—mightily.

When asked how he handles loss—when every possible option has been exhausted, with nothing left but pain—Tom reminds himself that, "This too shall pass."

"You feel bad right now? You feel pissed off? You feel angry? This too shall pass. You feel great? You feel like you know all the answers? You feel like finally everybody knows you? That everybody gets you? This too shall pass . . ."

Patience is a virtue. Time is your ally.

YOU ALWAYS THINK YOU COULD HAVE DONE BETTER

Queen's appearance at the 1985 Live Aid concert is widely regarded as one of the greatest live performances in rock history.

On July 13, 1985, at Wembley Stadium in London, Queen, fronted by the charismatic Freddie Mercury, performed a twenty-minute set, including such classics as "Bohemian Rhapsody," "Radio Ga Ga," "Hammer to Fall," "Crazy Little Thing Called Love," and "We Will Rock You." However, it was during their final song, "We Are the Champions," that Mercury had the crowd in the palm of his hand as he led them in a sing-along that has become legendary.

Thirty-eight years after the iconic set, Queen's lead guitarist, Brian May, was asked, "As you walked offstage after your Live Aid set in 1985, did you have any inkling that you'd just stolen the show?" May said,

> Heh! No. Absolutely no inkling whatsoever. You walk off things like that with a great feeling of exhilaration, but you're also doing the postmortem: "Oh, God, I didn't do that, I wish I'd done that, that went wrong."

This a familiar experience for any pro. The pro, as we say, is pleased but never satisfied. Even after a historic performance, the pro knows, specifically, what they could have done better. They do the postmortem. They break down the film. And they correct their mistakes the next time out.

KNOW WHO TO LISTEN TO

In 2020, I finished the season with the worst shooting percentage in my professional lacrosse career. The critics were all over me. They called out my shooting blunders—both with time and room and on the run. They said I wasn't what I used to be. They called my play selfish. They said I was washed up.

I also heard from analysts, players, and coaches who have expert game IQ. Even some of my opponents. They said: "You created your scoring chances, you registered assists and second assists." "You were beating your defender when you dodged." "You got back and played defense." "The only difference between this season and others . . . was your shots didn't fall."

Clarifying *the difference* was critical. If I hadn't registered record-breaking seasons in points and goals twice in my career, if I hadn't averaged more than a goal a game for over fourteen years—there would be no *difference*.

Your difference is what you're capable of—and I knew what I was capable of.

From there, I was able to ask for and receive better advice: Trevor Baptiste told me to focus more on dodging to my left as it was historically a higher percentage shot; Paul Carcaterra suggested that I sweep the middle to improve my shooting angle; and my assistant coach, Sean Kirwan, opened more time and room shooting chances by designing an off-ball cutting game plan to counter the defensive pressing I was getting.

It took me a while, but I had to discern who I listened to—and who to accept feedback from.

You have to be able to take the wise criticism and ignore the armchair experts on social media. You have to be able to sift through the noise to figure out what is and isn't accurate.

You have to know who to listen to.

HATERS ARE A TEST TO OVERCOME

You will have haters.

It takes time to sort through negativity. You have to build a relationship with it, set boundaries for yourself, and relearn to trust who you are and what you're doing.

I don't know a champion who doesn't have enemies. Jealousy and envy are core to the human gene. Let's get real . . . if you win a championship, you're now the last and only one standing. On the other side of any win are those who lose. They're not gonna like you.

Do you like losing? If you're like me, you must hate it.

So can you understand that when you become a champion, haters will be inevitable?

Now, let's look inward and work on ourselves. So far we've established that losing is a critical part of the journey for a champion—so let's be sure to designate how we're assigning our hatred of losing versus hatred of someone. They're different.

Don't be a hater.

A champion is no fool. When we lose, we look inward. We work harder, we analyze more critically, we ask questions, and we can't wait to get back out on the field for redemption.

You can dislike the way your competitor plays, how they talk shit, or the way they carry themselves. Fine. But I challenge you to recognize that they are serving a purpose in your journey—a test for you to overcome. Hating them is failing the test.

Beating them is the way.

YOU CAN SHUT YOUR EARS

Apparently, Winston Churchill hated the sound of whistling. He was once on a walk when a kid coming toward him was whistling loudly.

Churchill snapped, "Stop that whistling!"

"Why should I?" the kid said.

"Because I don't like it and it's a horrible noise."

"Well, you can shut your ears, can't you?"

"Churchill was for the moment stunned," one of his biographers writes. "Anger flushed his face." But then, he repeated what the kid said, "You can shut your ears, can't you?" and laughed out loud.

At some point in my career, it hit me that I had this power.

Remember, you choose who to listen to.

When the haters blasted me on social media . . . I shut my ears.

When the opponent was trying to get in my head . . . I shut my ears.

You have this power.

THE RIGHT SKIN THICKNESS

Sometimes, of course, the haters are right.

The journalist Derek Thompson is one of the best at what he does. In his writing, he explores everything from the history and future of work to the art and science of making things that a lot of people like. He has a knack for coining words and phrases that permeate culture. And for distilling complexity down into insights regular people can understand . . . and use.

But early in his career, Thompson couldn't take criticism. It didn't matter who it came from, Thompson writes, any bit of criticism "would always derail my day and send me into a spiral of self-doubt. I had thin skin."

Then, a few years into his career, Thompson read an interview with a famous journalist who, in Thompson's opinion, was getting worse and worse at writing. In the interview, the journalist said that the way they deal with criticism is by simply ignoring it altogether.

Thompson couldn't help but think, *No wonder you suck at writing now.* "This journalist had the opposite problem that I had," Thompson writes. "Their skin was too thick."

There is no "formula for growing one's 'ego epidermis' to the perfect level of thickness," Thompson writes. But "stay away from the extremes of hypersensitivity-to-feedback and obliviousness-to-feedback."

The season after I had the worst shooting percentage of my career, I finished with the best shooting percentage of my career.

I listened to the right people. I dodged more to my left, swept the middle, and cut off-ball.

GET OVER YOURSELF

I n the elimination game of the 1997 NBA Conference Semifinals, Kobe Bryant shot four air balls late in the game.

His team lost 98-93. He was asked how he handled this humiliating season-ending performance.

First, he told himself, "Get over yourself. You feel embarrassed? Get over yourself. You're worried about how people may perceive you? Get over yourself. You're not that important."

Second, he asked himself, "Why did those air balls happen?" Kobe was then a rookie, drafted straight out of high school. The year before, he played thirty-five games with plenty of rest time in between. In the NBA, there are eighty-two games in the regular season. So by the playoffs, Kobe said, "I didn't have the legs. If you look at those shots—every shot was on line, but every shot was short."

It was clear what he needed to work on: "I gotta get stronger. I gotta train differently. The weight training program that I'm doing—I gotta tailor it for an 82-game season, so that when the playoffs come around, my legs are stronger and that ball gets there."

It's a great two-step formula for bouncing back, whether from a bad season or a bad week at work. First, get over yourself. Detach from your ego, the part of you that feels embarrassed, that thinks others are thinking as much about your poor performance as you are. Then, analyze what went wrong and figure out what you have to do to come back better, stronger, faster, whatever it is.

TRUST THE LAW OF AVERAGES

I had at least one bad game every single season of my playing career. Even going back to my time in high school—there was a game where I shot 0 for 18. In college, every single season, there would be one, sometimes two games in a row where I would have zero points. In 2020, I started my season 0 for 12 and finished with the worst shooting percentage in my professional career.

At one point early in his career, Lou Gehrig hit a slump and nearly bounced out of the minor leagues. The owner of the Yankees sent a scout down to teach him a timeless lesson that all athletes have to learn. "The most important thing a young ball player can learn," the scout told Gehrig, "*is that he can't be good every day.*"

In the midst of one of my slumps, I had a conversation with Sue Bird. One of the greatest basketball players of this generation, Bird won eighteen championships around the world and dominated into her forties. She holds WNBA records for most assists, minutes played, All-Star appearances, and turnovers.

Like me, she'd have bad stretches. And when she was struggling from the field, she told me, she'd want to throw a tantrum about it.

This is her secret to getting back to a positive state of mind: "When I'm in a slump," she said, "at this point, I just put a lot of trust in the law of averages. I say to myself, 'Listen, you've been shooting this basketball for I couldn't even say how many years. And you've always been in the high thirties, low forties for three-point shooting percentage. That's who you are.' And so, I just put some trust in knowing *this is who I am.* And the only thing that's different is the way I'm thinking."

Not long before heading off to Rio de Janeiro for the 2016 Summer Olympics, long-distance runner Alexi Pappas had a bad workout. On a multi-mile run, her mile time was never below her target. She started to panic. Was she fatiguing right when she needed to be peaking?

"It's okay," her coach, a former Olympian himself, told Pappas. "It's just the rule of thirds."

Pappas asked, "What's the rule of thirds?"

"When you're chasing a dream or doing anything hard," Pappas explained, "you're meant to feel good a third of the time, okay a third of the time, and crappy a third of the time."

If the ratio is roughly in that range, you're good. As Pappas was—at those Rio games, she set Greece's national record in the 10,000 meters.

It's when you *always* feel crappy or you *always* feel good that you gotta look inward. If you're always feeling crappy, you might be burning out. If you're always feeling good, you might not be trying hard enough.

MAKE PEOPLE BETTER

Justin Herron was one of the best college football players in the country. He was a great athlete. He worked hard. He put up stats. He watched more film than anyone. He did well in the classroom.

So he was stunned when he wasn't voted captain of his Wake Forest team. He thought he had done everything right.

Justin's coach conceded, "Justin, you *do* do everything right . . . But football is a team sport. You need to set a good example and bring other guys with you."

Coach was right, Herron realized. He never thought about anyone's improvement but his own. He committed to changing that. After that meeting with his coach, Herron began to mentor younger players. Even the guys competing for his position—he took them under his wing. When he got injured, he typed up detailed breakdowns of the opponent for the guy who took his spot. When he went to watch film, he brought his teammates along with him. And after he graduated, he decided not to declare for the NFL Draft, instead returning as a grad student for one more season with his teammates.

And a year to the day, he got the call. "Congratulations, Justin," Coach said. "Your teammates have named you a team captain."

I'll always remember the class of captains I played with who committed to the other guys—Brodie Merrill, Ryan Boyle, Colin Doyle, Tucker Durkin, and Chris Watson. These men also shared one thing in common—they led at their best toward the end of their careers.

So I asked them why that was and they gave me two reasons. First, when you get older, you can physically impact the game less. Therefore, supporting your teammates becomes a bigger priority as it leads to a greater chance of winning. And second, maybe more naturally, you mature and become more observant. More reflective.

The way of the champion is not just a personal quest. It's not just about your own progress. It's not just about the heights you alone can reach. The effect you have on those around you is just as important—if not more so. Do you lift others up? Do you bring others along with you? Do you make people better?

That's what champions do. The champion makes people better. And they know their time will come.

LET OTHERS MAKE YOU BETTER

Throughout Michael Jordan's first five seasons with the Chicago Bulls, they had a run of back-to-back-to-back losing seasons, fired three head coaches, and were swept in the first round of the playoffs twice.

Then, in Jordan's sixth season, after a 21-point loss to the Detroit Pistons, the Bulls were sitting in ninth place in the conference, completely out of playoff contention. The day after the loss to the Pistons, Bulls' head coach Phil Jackson, as the *Chicago Tribune* reported, "named center Bill Cartwright a co-captain along with Michael Jordan, who had held the job by himself."

The Bulls won twelve of their next thirteen games. Then, after an eleven-game winning streak and a nine-game winning streak, they finished first place in their conference with a franchise-best 61-21 record. After sweeping the Knicks in the first round of the playoffs and knocking off the 76ers in just five games in the second round, the Bulls swept the Pistons in the Conference Finals. They lost Game 1 against the Lakers, then won the next four to win the 1991 NBA Finals.

As Sam Walker, author of *The Captain Class*, told me, "If you looked at the numbers, just purely the numbers, and asked, What's the moment the Bulls became a championship team? you would point to the day Cartwright was named co-captain. It was that day. It's clear as a bell."

When he stopped trying to do it all, when he stopped trying to put the team completely on his back, Sam said, "that's when Jordan became good."

"Bill," Jordan wrote of that 1990 season, "made all the difference."

After that devastating loss to Team Canada in 2014, a broken foot suffered two weeks later, capped by an offseason trade, sending me from Boston to New York, I met Brian Spallina. He was a six-time Major League Lacrosse champion defender who had the competitive streak and on-field presence of Bill Lambert. He was my co-captain.

In 2015, we won an MLL Championship—his record seventh as a pro.

Sometimes, being a great teammate is about lifting others up. Other times, it's about letting others help lift you up. You should be able to do anything, but you can't do everything.

FILL YOUR GAS TANK WITH PREMIUM

In late 2017, I was back in the town I grew up in for the holidays—Montgomery Village, Maryland. On Christmas Eve, after dinner with family, I went to a local gym to get a workout in.

There was only one other guy there. He was tall and looked athletic. He was doing resistance band exercises. About thirty minutes into my workout, he was still doing resistance band exercises. So I went over and struck up a conversation.

As it turned out, he played professional basketball in Europe. He was creeping up on his twentieth season in the pros. I started asking him about how to play at a high level for a long time.

"Here's what it is," he told me. "The pro athletes who stick around for a long time—they treat their bodies like Ferrari engines. For a decent amount of time, your high-performance car can run on regular fuel. But for longevity, it requires premium."

You, the driver, may not notice the difference between various types of gas—especially when you're young, or the car engine is new. But when your car starts to break down, it will break down fast, and you'll realize it's because you've been filling up the tank with regular unleaded fuel. Or, as you get older, if you're still performing at a high level, you'll know it's driven by the premium stuff.

"I still have a Ferrari," the man in the gym said. "I still fill the tank with premium. Sure, some days, I gotta go outside early in the morning, snow on the ground, start the engine, and let 'er warm up for a little while. But once the engine's going, I can compete with anyone."

If you want to play for a long time, this is what it takes.

When people ask me what I eat before games, I tell them the same thing that I eat every day—game or no game. To play well for a long time, you have to eat well for a long time. And hydrate. That's your fuel.

You will have to get to the facilities two to three hours before the younger guys, who can turn the keys and floor the gas immediately.

You will have to do resistance band exercises when the younger guys are lifting weights.

You will have to stick around and hit the ice baths when the younger guys jet out of the practice facilities straightaway.

Yes, you will have to make a ton of sacrifices. That's what it means to treat your body like a Ferrari engine. That's what it takes to compete at a high level for a long time.

REMEMBER YOUR PURPOSE

As a big-time college basketball coach, Shaka Smart has seen thousands of athletes make an interesting transition.

When athletes first step onto a college campus, suddenly they are no longer what they'd long been: the best.

Suddenly, they aren't the star player—or even a starting player. And before long, they are in Smart's office. It happens every year, he says. A player comes to him to say that they've lost their love for the game.

"I call bullshit on that in 99 percent of cases," Coach Smart said. "The love, the motivation, the drive—it's still in there. It's just being covered up by the stuff of life." It's just that what they thought they loved about the game was more the pleasure of winning, of being celebrated, of things coming easily.

All that is covered up now. By the new circumstances. By the pressures of academic responsibilities. By being asked to redshirt. By not getting playing time. By the distractions of schoolwork. By a toxic relationship. By the frustrations of putting in the same work without the recognition they're used to.

As you navigate the transitions to higher levels of competition, don't let the stuff of life fool you. Recognize that there will be challenges and distractions that might cloud your passion for the game. But the love, the intrinsic motivation that initially fueled that passion—it's still in there.

Remembering your purpose will help you get through these transitions. My purpose is to inspire and motivate others to push their physical and mental limits, to foster a culture of teamwork and dedication to the craft. I remember my twelve-year-old self who missed his first shot—which was embarrassing—then got back to work. I remind myself of the love I have for this game.

THE FOURTH MAN

I love how the NBA created an award for the first player off the bench—called the Sixth Man of the Year.

We put so much emphasis on making the team. After that, everyone wants to know, "Are you a starter?" Then it's "Are you an All-American? All-Pro? MVP?"

It never ends. The goalposts keep moving.

For me, it didn't stop at "starting." It quickly became about being the best player on my team, in the league, in the country, and in the world. I'm grateful for that competitiveness.

Though the real secret is committing to being the best at whatever, whenever, and wherever you're at.

In lacrosse, three midfielders, three attackmen, and three defensemen start. The fourth man would be the next one off the bench.

We don't have an award for being the best second-line midfielder. If we did, the fourth man might look like Manu Ginobli of the NBA. Sixth Man of the Year, then two-time All-NBA player, and four-time NBA champion.

It's essential to remember that success isn't solely about starting on the team, or being the star player. It's about making the most of every opportunity and excelling in the role you're given.

Tom Brady was the seventh-string quarterback at the University of Michigan, and he had a major problem. He was getting only two snaps at every practice. With that little to show for, how could he possibly prove to the coaches that he was worthy of climbing the depth chart? He was so frustrated that he almost transferred schools. His last-ditch effort was a trip to the team's sports psychologist, Greg Harden, where Brady told him, "I'm never going to get my chance. They're only giving me two reps." After some debate, they decided it didn't matter how many snaps Brady would get at the next practice—one, two, or ten. Rather, for every snap, Harden said that Brady must "Focus on doing the best you can with those two reps. Make them as perfect as you possibly can," Harden reminded him. From then on out, when Brady's name was called at practice, he would sprint out onto the field from the sideline and command a huddle as if it were the fourth quarter of the NFL Super Bowl. He brought the energy at the line of scrimmage, took under center perfectly, and handed the ball off seamlessly to the running back. The coaches took note. They wanted more energy and leadership in practice like Brady's. Soon, Brady saw his practice snaps go from two to twenty—now able to show his throwing ability and prowess for reading a defense.

Just like the Sixth Man on the San Antonio Spurs or the seventh-string quarterback at the University of Michigan, there are unpredictable players and moments in sports that will play a crucial role in the team's success.

THE WATER BOTTLE CARRIER

Sam Walker, author of *The Captain Class*, set out to answer one of the most hotly debated questions in sports: What are the greatest teams of all time? He devised a formula, applied it to thousands of teams from leagues all over the world, and when he was done, trimmed the best of the best down to a list of the sixteen most dominant teams in history.

With the list in hand, Walker became obsessed with another, more complicated question: What did these dynasties have in common? As he dug into their stories, a distinct pattern emerged: each team had the same type of captain—a singular leader with an unconventional skill set who was driven to achieve sustained, historic greatness.

He called this person the water bottle carrier. Relentless and always willing to put the needs of their teammates ahead of theirs. Rarely was this person the star player on the team. That person already had enough pressure on them each game to score. No, this person was a Carles Puyol—the center back for the Barcelona Football Club who helped his team win twenty-one titles across his ten-season captain campaign. Or a Carla Overbeck, captain of the United States women's national soccer team who would carry her teammates' bags to their hotel rooms even after a long international flight.

Just like anything in life, there's the perceived way, and there's the way that's studied, tested, and proven. The best teams in history had captains who did their best work behind the scenes. They often weren't the ones who scored dramatic points in the final minute of a big game, pulling off a heroic, game-saving win. Instead, they were chanting in the huddle with motivational firepower. They were true team-first leaders. They did the dirty work. They believed in one-on-one conversations versus generalized statements to the group at large.

One of the greatest footballers of all time—known as the King of

Soccer—is still the only player to have won three World Cups. And in 1958, 1962, and 1970, the captains for Brazil were Hilderaldo Bellini, Mauro Ramos, and Carlos Alberto.

I don't have to tell you his name and you know who he is—and he didn't *have* to be a captain to earn that level of respect and ubiquity.

LEAD BY EXAMPLE

Prior to the 2008 Olympics, the United States men's Olympic basketball team held a summer-long training camp in Las Vegas. The whole team stayed at the Wynn—a famous hotel on the Vegas Strip. On one of their first nights together, everyone except Kobe went out to the clubs.

"We were dressed to impress," Carlos Boozer said. "Got our fly stuff on. We had a good time." Dwyane Wade added, "That was so much fun."

It was a late one. The guys got back to the hotel around four thirty in the morning. When they walked into the lobby they saw Kobe with his gym bag, sneakers, and lifting gloves. He had just finished a workout in the hotel gym.

"This motherfucker Kobe was already drenched in sweat," LeBron James said. "And we was like, 'Yeah, he different.'"

The rest of the guys got in the elevator and as they headed up to their rooms, Boozer said, "We were all talking to each other, just like, 'This guy's really dedicated.'"

Pretty soon, it wasn't just Kobe going to the gym at four thirty in the morning. A couple of days later, LeBron and D-Wade were in there, too. "And by the end of the week," Boozer said, "the whole team was getting up every morning and were on Kobe's schedule."

One thing that separates a champion from everyone else is the ability to be consistently disciplined and uncompromising. This often creates the temptation to expect the same from others. But trying to hold others to the very same standards we hold ourselves to doesn't do anyone any good. It sets you up to be frustrated and disappointed. And it sets others up to be resentful.

Kobe didn't say anything to his teammates. He didn't make any comments about them hitting the clubs. He didn't impose his strict standards on them. He just let his actions do the talking. Head coach Mike Krzyzewski said, "That was his way of saying to the team, 'You can talk about things, but when you're actually doing it, you know, that's the main thing.'"

Tom Brady didn't have the arm strength to throw the ball 80 yards like JaMarcus Russell, nor could he run the 4.3 second forty-yard dash like Michael Vick. But he did have something inside of him that nobody could see from the outside. "Consistent discipline has been one of those prodigy-like strengths that I had," Brady said after he retired from the game.

Consistent discipline is *your superpower*. If you want others to be as dedicated as you are, to work as hard as you do, then communicate that entirely through your actions. Lead by example and you just may find yourself with an entire team in the weight room with you during off-hours.

THE 10-80-10 RULE

Duke lacrosse coach John Danowski was the head coach for our 2018 World Championship–contending Team USA. He had developed a relationship with his basketball colleague in Durham—one of the icons of coaching in hoops, Coach Mike Krzyzewski.

It was through that relationship with Coach Dino that we were able to meet Coach K—hear about his coaching philosophy, and even get a motivational pep talk twenty-four hours before our gold medal match against Canada in Netanya, Israel.

Let's talk philosophy.

He calls it the 10-80-10 rule. Coach surmises that at every level, in any discipline, from youth to pro, you have a bottom 10 percent of a team that's composed of players who are gonna cause problems, and you have an upper 10 percent of a team that's composed of players who are highly motivated, exceptionally gifted, and help set the culture of the team.

Coaches often spend most of their energy on the top and bottom 10 percent.

I've been on teams that were forced to run endless wind sprints before and after practice because two guys on our forty-six-man roster slept in and missed class that morning. You've probably heard the saying, "You're only as good as the last man on your roster"—the player who doesn't take many shifts in practice and doesn't step on the field in a game.

I've also been on teams where the coaches have obvious favorites. They spend most of their time with the best players on the team—thinking the only way to win big games is to have your best players step up in the big moments. Well, what happens if your best player fouled out, is in a shooting slump, or is getting double-teamed every time he has the ball?

In either case, both the bottom and top 10 percent want company. The problem starters often feel a sense of loneliness, thereby trying to convince more players on the team to join them on a Thursday night rendezvous to a downtown nightclub for a big night—having *just enough* time to recover

129

before that Saturday one o'clock game. The best and most committed on the team are pulling at the rest of the players to join them for midnight workouts and early film sessions with Coach—their best chance at gaining an edge for that Saturday game at one o'clock.

There's always a bottom and top 10 percent.

The best coaches in the world spend most of their time with the other 80 percent—the players who are most easily influenced to join either the top or bottom 10 percent.

TRUE LEADERSHIP

True leadership is not asking for anything that you haven't already done yourself.

Not a lift.

Not an extra sprint.

Not a second film session.

Not an early-morning workout.

Not a late-night practice.

True leaders lead by example.

IT'S A TEST

After a solid four years at Boston College, quarterback Matt Hasselbeck wasn't on the radar of many NFL teams. In fact, he wasn't invited to the NFL Combine. So his agent set up a Pro Day for him at BC. All thirty-two NFL teams were invited.

"Only one coach showed up," Hasselbeck told me. "The Green Bay Packers quarterbacks coach Andy Reid."

On that day, there was a blizzard and Boston College didn't have an indoor facility. "I guess we can't work out," Reid said, "since it's snowing." "No, no, no," Hasselbeck said. "We can still work out. I can throw in this."

It was a test, Reid said. "You passed. I'm not going outside in that snow. I just needed to know that you would be willing to go out and throw in that because I coach in Green Bay."

A couple of months later, with the 187th pick in the sixth round, the Packers drafted Hasselbeck. He went on to enjoy seventeen seasons in the NFL. He was selected to three Pro Bowls in his career, started in eleven playoff games (sixteenth all-time in NFL history), and led the Seattle Seahawks to Super Bowl XL.

The writer Michael Lewis is known to be good at getting to *really* know the people he goes on to write about in his books. Unlike most journalists, Lewis doesn't like to sit down with a subject, turn on a recorder, and ask a series of prepared questions. He prefers a version of a technique he picked up from his first job interview.

When he graduated from college, Lewis applied for a job to lead tour groups across Europe. He got an interview and when he showed up, the hiring manager said he didn't have time to do the interview because he was tasked with rearranging the office furniture. He asked if Lewis would help him. And for the next hour, Lewis moved furniture. Lewis got a call the next day—he got the job.

"It turned out he did this with everybody," Lewis said. "So the next guy or girl who went in for an interview, they moved the furniture back. Because he wanted to see how you'd respond." Because, Lewis said, "the seemingly trivial moments reveal a lot about a person."

Someone getting frustrated when asked to move furniture gives you a good sense of how they'll respond when things inevitably don't go exactly as planned on a tour across Europe. A player not wanting to work out because it's snowing tells you plenty about how they'll perform during a crucial late-season game on a cold, snowy day in December at Lambeau Field.

Everything is a test. Because how you do anything is an indication of how you do everything.

A TOUGH GUY

S port has conditioned me to be a tough SOB. On the field and off. But that toughness isn't spite. It's not hatred. It's competitive fire. It's heavily motivated and focused. And as Army Lacrosse head coach Joe Alberici taught me, it's inclusive.

Speaking to a group of kids, Coach Alberici explained that being inclusive means including "somebody who doesn't walk like you, talk like you, look like you—or doesn't have all the nice things that you have. Find that person. He's sitting by himself at a lunchtime table. Bring him over. Have him join your group. Be inclusive.

"Excluding people . . . that doesn't take much. That's not very tough."

I had the great pleasure of playing for Coach A in 2010 at the World Championships in Manchester, England. He was our offensive coordinator.

Five years earlier, as an assistant coach at Duke University, Coach Alberici and his wife gave birth to their son, Max, who was born eight weeks premature. He spent forty days in Duke's Neonatal Intensive Care Unit recovering from leukomalacia, an infant brain injury. Doctors weren't sure he would ever be able to walk. Shortly after, Max was diagnosed with cerebral palsy.

I remember celebrating a 12-10 gold medal–winning game over Canada—my first World Championship—and as we were getting ready to take a team photo from the stadium's Astro turf, Max came running over to me to join the picture. And that's the photo I have in my camera roll. Twenty-three guys, four coaches, and Max Alberici, wrapped around my shoulders.

After lacrosse was named to an all-new slate of competitions for the Los Angeles Olympics in 2028, I got a message from Max. He said, "Keep an eye out for any rumbling of anything to do with the Paralympic Games. You already know I will be on that team."

PRACTICE SMART

W atch a Steph Curry shooting workout. After he's done in the paint, he doesn't set up beside a rack of basketballs and shoot from one spot on the floor.

No. He runs off a pick, catches a pass, and shoots. He dribbles, drives, passes, runs to the corner, gets the ball back, and shoots. He dribbles between the legs, around the back, head fake, step back, and shoots.

This wasn't always the way he practiced, Steph told me. "I practice smart now," he said. "I'm not just in the gym just to be in there. There's a particular approach and mentality when I'm in the gym that I have to have every time. And that's a game speed mentality. Every hour, every minute I'm on the floor, I approach practice with that game speed mentality."

When I was younger, I went out and worked on my shot with a lot of wasted reps. I would go out and dump a bucket of balls in a spot and shoot for corners. I didn't think about if this was a shot I would take in a game— or the play that would need to happen before the shot opportunity.

I quickly realized that in games, I never scooped up a ball from ten yards out with the time and room to shoot as hard as I could. It was the opposite, really. I would catch a ball from a teammate, dodge my first defender, run as hard as I could down the alley, avoid a second sliding defender, then shoot on the run into a small window of open net.

When you go out to practice, you should work on the shots that you would take in a game.

That became me. Every shot I took was accounted for. There were stationary shots, shots on the run, shots taken off balance, and, most importantly, shots when I was tired and out of breath.

I learned how to put pressure into practice. Instead of getting endless opportunities to hit a corner, I would give myself three chances and run wind sprints against every shot I missed. I would hold myself accountable in practice, such that I didn't have a problem taking on the pressure in a game.

Practicing smart is about conditioning your behavior. It's about wiring your instincts. So that when you come off a pick and catch a pass, you're not thinking anymore.

"It's when nobody's watching in the gym," Steph told me, "that translates to confidence and success on the court."

SET GOALS YOU HAVE CONTROL OVER

A crucial moment in the 2009 World Series. The New York Yankees are up 2-1 in the series against the Philadelphia Phillies. Alex Rodriguez is at the plate in the top of the ninth inning with runners on first and third base. The game is tied 2-2. The count is 0-1. There are two outs. A-Rod rips a double to left field. One scores. The crowd erupts. Yankees win.

Twelve years later, I asked A-Rod about that moment.

"I made a paradigm shift on how I thought about big moments," he said. "In my first four or five years in the majors, I was always thinking about a transaction. I always wanted to have big stats. And I realized, that doesn't work. It's unrealistic."

In those early years, when A-Rod showed up at the ballpark, the expectation he set for himself was to go 3 for 4 at the plate, hit a home run, make a diving stop, and turn a double play.

The reality: he may get only three at bats, the other team may intentionally walk him all three times, and he may not get the ball hit toward him once. He was setting very unlikely, often impossible, expectations.

"I remember driving to the game," A-Rod continued, "and I just said to myself, 'In tonight's game, I just want to make the first play that presents itself to me. And then when I make that play, okay, I want to make the next play that presents itself to me.'"

The legendary basketball coach John Wooden would talk about "the fundamental goal." The goal in life is the same as in sports, he said: "Make the effort to do the best you are capable of doing. Make the effort to contribute in whatever way you can."

The stress that we feel often corresponds to poor, self-imposed expectations. We can alleviate that by focusing on making one play. "What that did for me," A-Rod said, "because the mind thinks in a singular way—it lowered the temperature, it decreased the pressure."

Make goals that you have control over. Make the first play that presents itself to you. Then the next one. And before you know it, you'll rip a double to left field in the ninth inning of the World Series.

COMPETE ONLY WITH YOURSELF

Comparison, it's said, is the thief of joy.

But it's hard to not compare yourself to others. It's hard to not compare your stats to the stats of the other team's best player. It's hard to not compare your title and wage to your colleagues at work. It's hard to not compare the number of followers you have on Instagram to the number of followers another player has. It's hard to not compare.

And it's hard to not feel the self-doubt inherent in feeling inferior to whoever it is you're comparing yourself to.

The legendary music producer Rick Rubin was asked if there's anything the artists he's worked with (which includes some of the all-time greats: Red Hot Chili Peppers, Tom Petty, Johnny Cash, Run-D.M.C., Eminem, Adele, Dr. Dre, and on and on) have in common.

They all struggle with self-doubt.

To overcome self-doubt, Rubin tells them, "Make it your goal to just be better than you were."

Make it your goal, he says, to focus on goals you have control over. "Compete only with yourself. If you say, 'I don't want to write unless I can write better than The Beatles,' that's a hard road. But if you say, 'I want to write a better song today than I wrote yesterday,' that can be done."

If you do that, if you consistently get better than you were, the rest will take care of itself.

PLAYING THROUGH INJURY

A t some point, we all get injured.

Late in the 2014 season, just after the World Championships, I suffered a Jones fracture in my left foot. I had season-ending surgery to repair it, then immediately began rehab.

By the start of the 2015 season, I was medically cleared to play. We got off to a blazing 8-0 start. During the All-Star break, I was in pain—so I got an eight-month post-op X-ray to see how my repaired bone was doing. They located a new stress fracture at the same site where I *just* had the original surgery—calling it a "nonunion fracture."

It was devastating. The doctors recommended that I shut it down for the rest of the season and fix my foot.

I had a decision to make.

Athletes have to weigh decisions relative to where they are in their careers. I was twenty-nine years old at the time. In sports, twenty-nine is old. With every season that passes, there's no guarantee you'll play the next. If you pass on an opportunity to be part of something special—like an undefeated championship team—there's no telling if that opportunity will come back around. If we were 0-8, I would have undergone surgery.

But we were 8-0.

So I made the decision to take some games off, then play through the injury for playoffs.

The pain was pretty constant. With my sports psychologist, John Eliot, I began working on different thinking and breathing techniques that helped me absorb and release the pain from injury. At halftime of games, our medical team would prearrange rehab near my locker, so as soon as I came in, I'd dunk my foot in ice, change out my orthotics, and retape. During the week, I worked with Johns Hopkins Hospital physical therapy specialist Ken Johnson, using a German-made shock wave system, hawk grips, and laser therapy to mend the fracture site and lessen the prior weekend's blow.

Our team was phenomenal. We won the championship.

Three days later, I flew down to Charlotte, North Carolina, to have my second foot surgery performed by Dr. Bob Anderson—widely recognized as the top foot and ankle surgeon in the United States.

At some point in their careers, most athletes face the same type of decision I had to make. Was it worth the risk? That's a difficult question to answer now because it happened to work out for me.

What should be accepted is that there is no right choice. The decision to play injured cannot be based on a desire to prove your toughness. It cannot be made because others are urging you to "tough it out" and "take one for the team." You can't ignore the long-term risks and repercussions.

It's a difficult decision, and it's yours alone to make.

GET UP AND DOWN

The key to success is your ability to endure.

Golf gets it right. Golf is an incredibly challenging sport, requiring a high level of mental aptitude and guts. It's here where I've learned how to create a "rebound goal."

In golf, great players master the up-and-down. Essentially, it means a player hits a tremendous shot . . . right after a terrible shot. Getting up and down means that you have to first make a mistake before you can have a stroke of genius.

Golf celebrates, rewards, and builds excitement around the up-and-down shot. Phil Mickelson has won tournaments and made millions of dollars from being widely known as the best up-and-down golfer on the tour.

In other sports, a bad shot or a bad play is usually followed by another bad one—then another and another. Because in other sports, we don't celebrate what happens after a bad shot or a bad play. Worse, some coaches have little tolerance for mistakes and won't give that player an opportunity to rebound.

Mostly, the coaches I played for gave us some leeway to take a bad shot or make a high-risk play. As such, I was able to focus on finding rebound opportunities when things didn't go as planned.

Rebounds that were within my control—being the first player back on defense after a bad shot, picking up a tough ground ball after a dropped pass, encouraging my teammates when we were losing—making the next play that presented itself.

Three-time Super Bowl–winning coach Bill Walsh writes in *The Score Takes Care of Itself* about the lowest point of his career. In his second season as head coach of the San Francisco 49ers, the team was on a seven-game losing streak heading into a week eleven matchup with the defending AFC East champion Miami Dolphins. An eighth-straight loss, Walsh knew, would put his job on a "death watch." In the final two minutes of the game, the 49ers had two field goals brought back because of holding penalties.

Then, out of field goal range, a fourth-down pass attempt came up short. They turned the ball over on downs, and lost.

Walsh said he would be forever haunted by that loss. On the long flight home, he sat alone and sobbed in the darkness. He considered resigning to save the embarrassment of getting fired. Then he thought about the following week's game against the New York Giants, which stirred something interesting inside him. "In my mind—or gut—and in spite of the pain, I knew I had to force myself to somehow start looking ahead," he writes. The awful feelings brought by the Miami loss started to retreat "because I was able to summon strength enough to pull my focus, my thinking, out of the past and move it forward to our next big problem."

Walsh and the 49ers won their next three games, including one of the greatest comebacks in NFL history—a 39-35 overtime win over the New Orleans Saints after trailing 35-7 at halftime. They took some of that momentum into the following season, and sixteen months after that loss to Miami, the San Francisco 49ers beat the Cincinnati Bengals 26-21 in Super Bowl XVI.

Mistakes, losses, failures are inevitable. It's what you do next that determines who you are. Do you compound the mistake? Or do you rebound?

It's time to get up and down.

THINK SMALL

To become a Navy SEAL, you have to complete BUD/S training—considered to be the most physically and mentally demanding military training program in the world.

Andy Stumpf, a retired Navy SEAL and SEAL instructor, was once asked about the number-one cause for SEAL candidates quitting during BUD/S.

Stumpf said he would always ask people when they quit, "Why? You said this is your lifelong goal, this is all you ever wanted to do . . . and you quit. Why?"

"Time and time again," Stumpf said, "the answer I got from students was they got overwhelmed." They didn't keep "their world small," Stumpf said. "There's two ways you can look at BUD/S. It's 180 days long. Or you can look at it as a sunrise and a sunset, 180 times."

Stumpf said that early on, he got the best advice: "Just make it to your next meal because they have to feed you every six hours," he was told. "It doesn't matter how much I'm in pain, doesn't matter how cold I am . . . just get to the next meal."

When the Roman emperor Marcus Aurelius was overwhelmed by the enormity of his responsibilities, he would remind himself, "Don't let your imagination be crushed by life as a whole." Think small, he was saying, "stick with the situation at hand."

When the writer Ernest Hemingway was overwhelmed by the enormity of a book project, he would remind himself, "All you have to do is write one true sentence. Write the truest sentence that you know."

BUD/S, an emperor's to-do list, writing a book—most things of magnitude are really just a series of small component parts. The way through is to simply focus on those small component parts. Just get to the next meal. Just knock off one item on the to-do list. Just write one true sentence. Run hard onto the field during your next shift. Think small.

CONSISTENCY IS THE DIFFERENCE

José Mourinho, widely thought to be among the best coaches in football, had a tough-love conversation with Dele Alli. Alli was once regarded as the most exciting young talent in the game. But he wasn't reaching his full potential. So Mourinho called Alli into his office.

As Alli's coach, Mourinho said, "I have to tell you always what I think. Maybe you will tell me to fuck off, but I have to tell you exactly what I've seen. And for me, since the beginning, I had no doubts about your potential."

Alli has had incredible moments, Mourinho says. Incredible matches. Flashes of greatness.

But, Mourinho says, "there is a huge difference between a player that keeps consistency and the player that has moments. And that is what makes the difference between a top player and a player with top potential."

Consistency is the difference. Demanding more from yourself. Putting in the hard work. Making the sacrifices that others won't. There's a reason why most athletes are just players with top potential. As Mourinho says, "Time flies."

In sport, you have a small window of time to play and reach your full potential.

The way of the champion is to be able to say, on the day you hang 'em up, that you put in the hard work, you made the necessary sacrifices, and you were a top player.

THE AB WORK

There will be days when you don't want to get out of bed. You won't want to train. You won't want to go out and get your one hundred shots in.

These are great days. Because these are the days champions get to separate themselves from everyone else.

"There were a lot of days where I did not want to get out of bed," Michael Phelps said of his legendary swimming career. "But if you look at the greats in any walk of life, the greats do things when they don't always want to. And that's the separation."

I haven't met many athletes who like to do ab workouts. They're long and painful—putting you on your back and out of breath. It's a marathon. They typically come at the end of a hard-core workout when you're already exhausted. I've never seen an exercise skipped more often than crunches, planks, and mountain climbers.

What does that tell you?

That's where the gold is. That's where the growth is. That's where the separation is.

In sports, in business, and in life, the things that are most avoided are where the most advantage is.

Don't want to do abs? Fine. You'll be more injury-prone and less explosive.

Don't want to prospect new leads late at night? Fine. You'll miss your revenue goals.

Don't want to have that hard conversation with your partner? Fine. The relationship will harbor resentments and won't last.

Abs represent the work that most people won't do. So commit to doing the ab work, and watch as you improve at a rate that others won't.

PRESSURE IS A SIGNAL

When he was just a kid in Oakville, Ontario, John Tavares showed enough promise for hockey fans to dub him "the next Wayne Gretzky." Talk about pressure.

That's the story of Tavares's career: dealing with pressure.

When he was fourteen, Tavares put up eighty-three goals and sixty-four assists in a AAA minor hockey league season. It was so unheard of that for the first time ever, the Ontario Hockey League (OHL) broke its age-limit policy and granted Tavares eligibility for the OHL entry draft. The news spread and all eyes were on Tavares—*Was the kid really worthy of breaking the rules? Was he really that "exceptional"?*

Tavares scored ten goals in his first nine OHL games, finished his first season with 77 points, and was named OHL Rookie of the Year. In year two, "the next Wayne Gretzky" scored seventy-two goals and broke The Great One's record for most goals by a sixteen-year-old in the OHL. Tavares finished his stint in the OHL with 215 goals (OHL record) and 218 assists. And, no surprise, he was drafted first overall by the New York Islanders in the 2009 NHL Draft.

Fast-forward, after nine big seasons with the Islanders, Tavares took an opportunity to live out his childhood dream of playing for his hometown team, signing with the Toronto Maple Leafs. In his second season with Toronto, Tavares was named captain of the Leafs, a position so important to the organization that they hadn't filled it in over three years.

As thirteen-time Stanley Cup champions, the Leafs carry with them a legacy matched by only a few teams around the world. In the city of Toronto, the captain of its historic franchise isn't just a leader on the ice, he's also the face of the city.

More pressure.

It was a year into this role that I talked to Tavares about it. "The way I look at pressure," he told me, "is that pressure is a gift that gives you a rare opportunity to do something special. Pressure signals that what you're doing has incredible meaning and purpose."

The person to pity is not the person who has a lot of pressure on them, but the person who has never had pressure on them. That person has never had the chance to do anything special.

You don't get nervous before a preseason game against a lousy opponent. You don't get butterflies driving to the office on a routine day. You don't get jitters before stepping out for an afternoon jog.

No.

You get nervous before a big game. You get butterflies driving to the office on the day of an important presentation. You get jitters before stepping on the ice as the leader of one of the most storied franchises in hockey.

Legendary coach to some of the greatest tennis champions, Nick Bollettieri shared both an empathetic and direct take on the nerves he's seen his best players work through. "Champions find a way to get through their nerves. Don't be embarrassed to say that you're nervous. Everyone is nervous. But [champions] find a way to get over it," he said.

Pressure and nerves are signals telling you that what you're doing is important. It's the gift of a rare opportunity. It's the chance to do something special.

And that's an awesome place to be. Embrace it.

EFFORT OVER OUTCOMES

In a twelve-year stretch, the legendary college basketball coach John Wooden won ten NCAA championships. In that period, his teams won a record eighty-eight consecutive games.

The teams coached by John Wooden, in other words, were cool under pressure—impossible to rattle.

His players were skilled and well-conditioned, but lots of teams had that. Wooden said they performed under pressure the way they did not because of their strategy, skill, or fitness, but rather because of the way he defined success for the team.

"Success is peace of mind," Wooden taught everyone he coached, "which is a direct result of self-satisfaction in knowing you made the effort to become the best that you are capable of becoming."

But the key, Wooden writes, was getting his players not just to agree that effort matters more than outcomes, but to believe it. Once you believe it, you don't fear losing, you don't think or care about what the fans or the media might say, you don't get nervous about what the opponent might do. A team full of players who define success this way "will not break down, get rattled, or succumb because of nerves."

Our 2010 gold medal–winning coach with Team USA, Mike Pressler, insisted that I not be outcome-oriented. In an effort to further persuade my twenty-four-year-old self, Coach P told me that "the script has already been written"—so get back to the page that we're in right now. The practice. The ground ball. The opening face-off.

That gave me peace of mind.

The reward for putting in the work is not just what shows up on the stat sheet, in the win-loss column, or on the trophy shelf. It's the peace, the contentment, the satisfaction of knowing you've done all you can, which permeates everything you do and everywhere you go.

FINDING YOUR NEW HUNGER

Gregg Popovich, the all-time winningest coach in NBA history and five-time NBA champion, talked about how the first championship is the easiest to win.

Before the first one, every team's temperament is built around not having won. For an athlete, there's no greater fuel. Everything you do is driven by that desire to get to the top.

But what happens when you get there?

After the first championship, Popovich said, the most foolish thing he could have done was to go back to his players and expect the same offseason hunger. I've been on teams that were led that way. As if we could possibly convince ourselves that we hadn't won the championship. It's a poor use of energy and mindset.

I've won championships at every level—high school, college, professionally, and internationally—which mostly means that I've played on extraordinarily talented teams. And after each championship, we had to accept a new reality. You have to find your new drive, a new reason. It's not about proving yourself a champion anymore—the ring, the trophy, and the final standings proved that.

Every champion finds a new reason to keep going just as hard as before. Perhaps it's the hunger to go back-to-back—one of the rare occurrences in team sports. Maybe it's silencing the rest of the league who called it a fluke. Whatever reason, it's time to do it on your terms now.

When the hunger to do something for the first time is sated, how will you create a new hunger that's just as strong?

S uper Bowl LI will go down not just as one of the great Super Bowls, but as one of the great sporting events of all time.

It was the New England Patriots vs. the Atlanta Falcons. The Patriots finished the regular season with an NFL-best 14-2 record. It was the Patriots' seventh Super Bowl appearance in the Tom Brady–Bill Belichick era. The Falcons—led by the regular-season NFL MVP, quarterback Matt Ryan—made it to their second Super Bowl in franchise history.

When I was a freshman at Johns Hopkins, nobody on the team had won a college championship. In fact, the all-time winningest program in college lacrosse history hadn't won an NCAA championship in eighteen years. We had the desire to win at all costs. That never-won-before fuel is a formidable fuel. The Falcons had that fuel. The Patriots had to find theirs. And for the first half, the Patriots couldn't find it.

The Falcons jumped out to a 21-0 lead. With two seconds left in the first half, the Patriots kicked a field goal before they went into the locker room down 21-3.

"The locker room at halftime was quiet," Patriots tight end Martellus Bennett told me. Marty stepped in midseason when All-Pro tight end Rob Gronkowski suffered a season-ending injury. He quickly became one of Tom Brady's favorite targets. Heading into the Super Bowl, Marty was already leading the Patriots in touchdown receptions. After a slow first half offensively, Marty sat in the locker room thinking Brady would be looking for him more and more in the second half.

"Everyone was focused," Marty continued. "I didn't see anyone lose hope. I was looking around at everyone, and everyone was just focused on themselves. I could tell that everyone was thinking, 'What could I do? What could I do to help the team?' No one came in going, 'You need to fucking do this.' Or, 'It's your fucking fault.' Or, 'You motherfuckers gotta step it up.' Coaches didn't do it. Players didn't do it."

Then, Marty was told what he could do to help the team. The Falcons' defense was putting a lot of pressure on Brady. "We want to tighten down on the inside," Marty was told. "So we're gonna need you to chip a lot more in the second half."

A tight end like Marty—who typically hauls in a lot of receptions—doesn't necessarily want to chip-block in the Super Bowl. A chip block means that before the tight end can run their route, they have to stall and try to hit a pass rusher. It makes it harder for the tight end to get open before the quarterback needs to get the ball out. Essentially, a tight end who is asked to chip is a tight end who is not going to catch any passes.

"But I was like, 'All right, if that's what you need me to do, I'll do it,'" Marty told me. "Who gives a fuck who catches the ball in the Super Bowl? The ultimate goal is to win the fucking Super Bowl."

In the week leading up to the big game, the Patriots practiced for the season's longest Super Bowl halftime show. They studied what they wanted to do with the fifteen additional minutes of waiting on Lady Gaga's performance in front of a hundred million fans watching at home. Coach Belichick would instruct his players to leave the practice field, head into the locker room, and wait. Once the clock hit zero, Coach would bring the players back out to practice. Brilliant.

Before running back onto the field for the second half, Marty said the only thing he remembers hearing was everyone echoing Coach Bill Belichick's now-famous mantra: "Do *your* job."

Don't worry about what anyone else is doing. Focus on doing what the team needs *you* to do. When your number is called, do your job.

"They asked me to chip," Marty said. "I was chipping the fuck out of people."

At one point, Marty chip-blocked the Falcons' defensive end Dwight Freeney so hard that their helmets got stuck together. "There were points where I didn't even know what happened on the play because I was so focused on my job."

This is the way of the champion. They do what the team needs them to do. Sometimes, it's scoring touchdowns. Other times it's chip blocking. Sometimes it's putting the team on your back. Other times it's putting them ahead of you and pushing them forward.

This is how, against the odds, the Patriots would come back to win that game in one of the greatest victories in all of sports history.

In 2005, Johns Hopkins University won its first NCAA Championship in eighteen years. Part of that season's success was fueled by our desire to win our first ring. Part of it was fueled by a determination to bring Hopkins lacrosse back to the top. And part of it was fueled by a heightened sense of focus for every player to do their fucking job. No more, no less.

Tiger Woods played in his first PGA Tour event at the Riviera in 1992— he was sixteen.

At the time, nobody could have imagined how high Tiger would rise, but what they could see was how remarkably smooth his swing was. It was like silk.

In 1996, Tiger won his first career PGA Tour event at the Las Vegas Invitational, and the rest was history. He won the 1997 Masters, and over the next four years brought home another forty PGA Tour wins and another seven Major Championships—including two more Masters, two PGA Championships, two U.S. Opens, and The Open Championship.

Tiger, widely regarded as one of the greatest golfers in the history of the sport, has consistently demonstrated a relentless pursuit of improvement. Into his twenties, he began getting stronger, started swinging faster—with new muscle load and equipment changes that included lighter driver heads and shafts, and more aerodynamic balls. As a player who could outdrive everyone with a better short game than anyone, you would think that Tiger would have chosen to keep the momentum going.

No. At twenty-eight years of age, considered by many to be the greatest athlete walking the planet, backed by an historic run of championships, Tiger decided to hire a new swing coach, Hank Haney—tasking him with rebuilding his entire swing. Undergoing this change felt way too risky for many golf analysts around the world. Tiger was on his way to hanging in the rafters with Jack Nicklaus, but if his swing change went wrong, he could have thrown it all away.

Haney recalled Tiger's fear of "the big miss." With such power, Tiger was concerned with pulling the ball right or cutting the ball left—leading to bogey or worse. In his book *The Big Miss: My Years Coaching Tiger Woods*, Haney reminds us that Tiger's swing reconfiguration was not done overnight. He spent "one hundred fifty days a year with him for six years."

Haney worked to open Tiger's club position at the top of his swing, which was less closed across the line so he could take advantage of a faster motion that accompanied his newfound strength. There was less of a pause between Tiger's backswing and downswing, lowering his margin for error—where he might drive the ball right or left. This was a new tempo that would propel Tiger to eighty-four more PGA Tour wins, and eight Major championships.

That's the way of the champion. Whether in sports, business, or life, the greats are known for how they're always looking to add a new element to their game. They're eager to navigate the intricacies of transformation, fine-tuning their technique.

Everyone is skilled and talented. The differentiator becomes: Who keeps looking to add to their game? Who doesn't linger comfortably with their current ability? Who doesn't feel satisfied with their current success? Who never stops working to get better?

The best reinvent their swing. Over and over and over.

YOU SHOULD ENJOY IT

Right after winning a championship in 2011, I said something on live television that I wish I hadn't.

I was asked a classic post-championship win question. *How does it feel?* And I gave a classic post-championship win answer: *Feels great. We're going to enjoy this one. But . . . get back to work tomorrow.*

The top performers in the world have an insatiable appetite. To reach the heights of success, you often carry with you a never-enough mentality. It's hard to turn off, so a lot of us miss out on opportunities to enjoy the fruits of our labor.

Speaking at Philadelphia's University of the Arts, the prolific multi-genre writer Neil Gaiman told the story of the best advice he was ever given, which he failed to listen to.

Once, at the height of the success of his comic book series *The Sandman*, Gaiman was with another all-time great writer, Stephen King. King could see the excitement surrounding *The Sandman*—the rave reviews, the long lines at Gaiman's book signings, all that sort of stuff.

King's advice to Gaiman was this: "This is really great. You should enjoy it."

"And I didn't," Gaiman said. "Best advice I ever got but I ignored. Instead, I worried about it. I worried about the next deadline, the next idea, the next story. There wasn't a moment for the next fourteen or fifteen years that I wasn't writing something in my head, or wondering about it. And I didn't stop and look around and go, 'This is really fun.' I wish I'd enjoyed it more."

I'm glad I got back to work. I'm glad I didn't rest on my laurels. I also wish I'd enjoyed it more. I wish I had allowed myself to sit in the moment and fully embrace the achievement and joy of winning a championship. I wish I hadn't perpetuated the idea that the only thing to be thinking about at the top of the mountain is getting to the next peak. Because it isn't.

You can be present. You can be grateful. You can be happy. And with all of that, you can still be hungry.

BE OBSESSED WITH NOT MISSING IT

The movie *The End of the Tour* was one of the most anticipated films of the 2015 Sundance Film Festival. Critics had been raving about the performance of the film's star, Jason Segel.

When Segel arrived in Salt Lake City for Sundance that year, his friend said to him as they got off the plane, "Be present for all of this. You are not going to post-enjoy it."

Segel says he thinks about that advice all the time. Like when he's at a concert and sees people with their phones out the whole time, filming. "If you're not enjoying the stuff while it's happening, you're missing it. I've become obsessed with not missing it. There's a lot that I look back on and think, 'Man, you missed it.' And I never wanna miss it again."

Lyle Thompson grew up in the Onondaga Nation. He was one of five children, playing lacrosse in the backyard, without a net. The Thompsons couldn't afford one. All of Lyle's equipment was passed down, yet he became the number-one high school recruit in the country . . . as a sophomore. He went on to set the all-time points record in NCAA Division 1 lacrosse history, win a Tewaaraton Award (our sport's Heisman Trophy), and become a pro lacrosse MVP.

His legacy of success on the field will live on for generations. But, as he said in *Fate of a Sport*, all that is worthless without presence:

> You can win all of the championships in the world, but if you weren't present doing it, what was it worth? If you aren't having fun while you were doing it, what was it all worth?

> You can be the talk of the festival, but if you weren't present for it, what was it worth?

> You can travel to every corner of the globe, taking pictures every step of the way—but if you weren't present in the moment, you missed it. Sure,

you can be excited about the day when your kid can drive themself to their friend's house, but don't let looking to the future get in the way of enjoying this moment—right now, with your kid in the back seat smiling at you.

You can achieve all the material success in the world, but if you weren't present during the journey, you missed it.

THIS AIN'T GONNA LAST

October 16, 2010. The Rutgers Scarlet Knights vs. the Army Black Knights. MetLife Stadium, one of the biggest venues in the heart of the sports capital of the world.

Late in the fourth quarter, Rutgers is down 17-10. They score on a 16-yard touchdown pass to tie it up. On the ensuing kickoff, Eric Le-Grand's life changed forever. He ran down the field, split through a double team, and had Army's kickoff returner perfectly lined up for a big tackle. "When you've run down the field as many times as I had," LeGrand told me ten years later, "you can judge when it's going to be a big hit, and you try to prepare your body for that."

He and the Army player were running straight at each other. Preparing his body for a big straight-on tackle, LeGrand decided to lead with his shoulder, to keep his head completely out of it.

But a split second before LeGrand got there, one of his teammates got a piece of the Army player's leg, just enough to trip him up and change his trajectory. Instead of his shoulder, the crown of LeGrand's head went into the back of the Army player's shoulder blade.

Seconds later, LeGrand lay on the 25-yard line, surrounded by Rutgers trainers. They asked him if he could move or feel anything when they put pressure on his legs. All LeGrand could do was say, "I can't breathe." A few minutes later, he was put on a stretcher, and as he was lifted onto a cart, he caught a gasp of air. "So I thought I had just knocked the wind out of myself," he told me. "So I'm thinking, 'Okay, this is just a full-body stinger. Everything will come back in a few minutes. I'll be all right.'"

He was carted off the field.

"I heard the crowd clapping. I went to give the thumbs-up to let everyone know I was going to be okay. And when it didn't move, it was pretty scary." He said it felt like a thousand-pound cinder block was preventing him from giving the thumbs-up.

LeGrand was rushed to the intensive care unit of the Hackensack University Medical Center. There, doctors determined that LeGrand was paralyzed from the neck down. He had fractured his C3 and C4 vertebrae. He was told he would never be able to come off a ventilator and he had 0 percent chance of walking again.

A month later, he was off the ventilator, able to breathe on his own.

LeGrand then transferred to Kessler Institute for Rehabilitation, one of the leaders in spinal cord rehabilitation, and began the arduous process of physical therapy.

Two years later, at the 2012 ESPY Awards, in his speech after receiving the Jimmy V Award for Perseverance, LeGrand said that he would someday walk again. Ten years later, LeGrand continues to work toward defying those 0 percent odds.

How does he keep at it? How does he hold on to optimism more than a decade into his recovery? How does he get through the bad days, the mental downward spirals, the thoughts of doubt and frustration and "what if" and "why me"?

"It's the mental toughness I picked up as an athlete," he told me. "Those times on the field, those weight room and conditioning sessions, your coach is in your face, you feel like you're gonna break, you feel like you can't do it, you can't go any further—and you overcome it. That feeling of joy after you get through such a tough moment—I try to remind myself of that. When I'm down, when I'm going through a tough time, I'm frustrated, I'm doubting—I say, 'This ain't gonna last, E. You got this. You can push through this.' And then once you get over it, once that time passes, you feel good, stronger, for having gotten through it."

The good, the bad, the beautiful, even the tragic and terrifying—all events of the world flow past us quickly. None of them are stable. Each of them disappears with due time. Everything must pass.

When you're down, going through a tough time, frustrated, or doubting, always remember: this ain't gonna last, E.

And when it does pass—because it will—you'll be better for having gotten through it.

BOOK 3 BEYOND THE GAME

The man who views the world at fifty the same way he did at twenty has wasted thirty years of his life.

—MUHAMMAD ALI

A real champion measures not just stats, but impact. Impact on their teammates, on their community, on their sport—not just locally, but globally. Off the field, champions do things for the good of the game. They make sacrifices. They make unpopular decisions. They fight. And not just for the game—but for their family, their community, their peers, the world. This is what is required of you now. You have to take your talents and influence beyond the game, becoming an ambassador for the values and principles that elevate the sport and inspire others. Embrace the responsibility that comes with greatness and use your platform to effect positive change. Leave a lasting legacy that extends far beyond the scoreboard. Remember, a true champion's impact is not just measured in trophies and accolades but in the lives they touch, the minds they inspire, and the positive change they bring to the world.

THE SECOND MOUNTAIN

After retiring from professional baseball, Lou Gehrig was appointed to New York City parole commissioner. He was a living legend, someone who could have made a financial killing with speaking engagements and guest appearances. Instead, the final two years of Gehrig's life were spent in the service of others.

After retiring from professional basketball, David Robinson established the Carver Academy in San Antonio, Texas, to provide educational opportunities for underprivileged children.

After retiring from professional football, Jim Brown became a civil rights activist, founded the Black Economic Union to help minority-owned businesses, and even helped establish the Watts truce—a peace agreement between rival Los Angeles gangs.

After her Olympic gymnastics career, Kerri Strug got a master's degree in social psychology from Stanford University before joining the Justice Department's Office of Juvenile Justice and Delinquency Prevention.

After his professional boxing career, Manny Pacquiao was elected to the House of Representatives and then the Senate in his home country of the Philippines.

After retiring from professional tennis, Arthur Ashe became a vocal civil rights activist and advocate for social justice. He focused on promoting education and health initiatives, particularly for underprivileged children. Ashe also established the Arthur Ashe Foundation for the Defeat of AIDS to raise awareness and funds for AIDS research.

After his professional basketball career, Kobe Bryant was prolific in his tragically cut-short second act. He won an Academy Award for Best Animated Short Film for *Dear Basketball*, which he wrote and narrated. He wrote several books. He granted over two hundred requests for the Make-A-Wish Foundation. He started the Kobe and Vanessa Bryant Family Foundation, "helping young people in need, encouraging the development of physical and social skills through sports and assisting the homeless." And he founded the Mamba Sports Academy, "educating and empowering the next generation of kids through sports."

These athletes—and many others—climbed what the prominent journalist and author David Brooks calls the Second Mountain.

The First Mountain is what we've been focused on for the first two thirds of this book. It's the pursuit of individual goals, personal success, and team achievements. It's the path we've followed as we strove to establish our careers, accumulate wealth, achieve recognition, and pursue personal happiness. As we climbed the First Mountain, success was often measured by external markers such as wealth, status, awards, and championships.

Now, we shift our focus, our energy, our resources, our knowledge and skills to climbing the Second Mountain. It involves moving away from self-centered pursuits and turning toward service, relationships, community, and causes larger than oneself. It's finding purpose, satisfaction, and fulfillment through acts of service and giving back to the community. It's living a life centered on a sense of responsibility to others, looking beyond ourselves and considering the greater impact we can have on our communities and the world.

Those who shift their focus to this Second Mountain find deep fulfillment and purpose in life after sports. Through acts of service, they create a positive legacy, one that impacts more people and lasts far longer than what they did as professional athletes. And in doing so, they are no longer pros. They become champions.

YOU STILL CAN'T MISS A DAY

E ven after you retire . . . you still can't miss a day.

Even after you retire . . . one hundred shots.

After you launch your new venture . . . one hundred shots.

After back-to-back-to-back meetings . . . one hundred shots.

After you have your first child, sell your first company, make your first million . . . one hundred shots.

I keep a collapsible goal in my car. I love shooting on net, hitting the wall, and introducing people to the sport of lacrosse. Before a big investor meeting, I get a hundred shots. Before a live TV hit, a hundred shots. Before PLL games, like Mark Cuban does at the American Airlines Center in Dallas . . . one hundred shots.

For as long as my body allows, I will get my hundred shots.

Keep playing the game you love. Keep getting up shots. Keep the stick in hand. Keep a ball in the office. Keep the cleats in the trunk. Keep not missing a day.

FROM ME TO YOU

Songs on the Beatles' debut album include first-person pronouns.

"Please Please Me"
"Love Me Do"
"P.S. I Love You"
"I Saw Her Standing There"

Then as the Beatles got more and more successful, they made a subtle shift. "We were new to the whole idea of fans," the Beatles' Paul McCartney explained. As they were becoming aware of all the people listening to their music, McCartney and his bandmate and writing partner John Lennon wrote their third single, "From Me to You." The song was the Beatles' first number-one hit on the UK singles chart.

"It was directed at our fans," McCartney said.

It was the shift from the First to the Second Mountain, an intentional movement from the self ("me") to the community ("you").

Just as the Second Mountain represents a stage of giving back, service, and building meaningful connections with others, the Beatles' shift reflects a desire to engage more deeply with their audience and establish impact beyond just personal creative fulfillment. This transition demonstrates their growth as artists and individuals.

As we move beyond being a pro into becoming a champion, we make this same move: *from me to you.*

GOING FOR IT

In the movie *Jaws*, you don't actually see the shark until an hour and twenty-one minutes into the film. It goes to show, things can often be scarier in our imaginations than in reality.

In every game I played, I experienced nerves of anticipation right up to the opening face-off. And then, the whistle blows—boom, the nerves are gone. I'm in the moment.

This is how it goes off the field as well. As we think about starting a company or uploading an article online, as we think about asking our boss for a raise or an attractive stranger out on a date, as we think about stepping into the unknown—we psych ourselves out, anticipating the different, often cynical ways in which reality might unfold.

Remember, you know what you're doing. Legendary NFL head coach Chuck Noll would remind his players, "Pressure is what you feel when you don't know what you're doing." He led the Pittsburgh Steelers from 1969 to 1991, one of the longest tenures in NFL history. He had seen it all. Nerves are natural. They mean you care.

A champion doesn't experience these nerves less often than the average person. Rather, we don't give in to them. We learn to live with them. We get up and close with them. We don't let them prevent us from starting, from asking, from stepping into the unknown.

Knowing that things are scarier in our imagination than reality, we go for it.

YOU NEED A GOOD STORY

t's one of the most iconic photographs of all time. Muhammad Ali underwater in a perfect boxing pose.

In 1961, a freelance photographer named Flip Schulke and Ali met for the first time. Ali had recently won a gold medal at the Summer Olympics. "To impress him," Schulke writes, he showed Ali some underwater waterskiing photos he had published in *Life* magazine.

After Ali saw the underwater photos, he told Schulke to meet him at the Sir John Hotel the next day. When Schulke showed up, Ali was already in the pool, training in the shallow end. "He was doing a hook and a jab," Schulke writes. "I said to him, 'That's fantastic because I see your fists going through the water, like my water-skiing pictures.' And he said to me, 'Oh, I've always done this.'"

Ali said his first trainer taught him that "if I practice in the pool, the water resistance acts just like a weight." Since then, Ali said, he'd been doing this pool training.

No wonder Ali is so fast in the boxing ring, Schulke thought.

Yeah, Ali said, "that comes from punching under water . . . You try to box hard. Then when you punch the same way out of water, you got speed."

Makes sense.

Schulke forgot his bathing suit, but Ali had an extra pair of boxing shorts. Schulke put them on and joined Ali in the shallow end of the pool.

"He was standing on the bottom of the pool," Schulke later said, "in a perfect boxing pose. . . . I got about six pictures of him. He was holding his breath all this time and not making any movement."

Schulke's piece ran in *Life* magazine on September 8, 1961. The story of Ali's underwater training regimen traveled around the world.

Three years later, Schulke writes, "I went back to photograph him again."

Schulke was showing Ali a scrapbook of the photos he had taken since their hotel pool shoot.

"When he came across my underwater pictures he winked at me," Schulke writes.

It turned out Muhammad Ali didn't actually train in a pool. He didn't even know how to swim. He just thought it would be a good story.

"He fooled me," Schulke writes. "He fooled everybody."

In 1964, Phil Knight and his college track and field coach, Bill Bowerman, started Blue Ribbon Sports—later named Nike. Then, the total addressable market for athletic shoes was tiny. That's because only amateur and professional athletes were buying footwear to run in. That is until 1966, when Bowerman published the book *Jogging: A Medically Approved Physical Fitness Program for All Ages Prepared by a Heart Specialist and a Famous Track Coach*. Immediately, the book became a bestseller. *Life* magazine and *The New York Times* featured massive stories on the new phenomenon, writing "Jogging is an 'in' sport." The book quickly sold over one million copies across the United States.

Nike wasn't the first or best shoe on the market. They were the ones who made jogging in America cool. Bill Bowerman was the one who told his cofounder that, "If you have a body, you are an athlete." Today, Nike sells twenty-five pairs of shoes per second, earning $100 million in sales per day, amounting to over $46 billion in 2022.

Part of the journey is having a good *story*.

Part of my *story* was becoming lacrosse's first millionaire. Sure, the sum of my sponsorship deals were worth that over several years—but I wasn't making a million bucks a year standalone. It was the label, "Lacrosse's Million Dollar Man," that meant something. It was now a *Bloomberg* magazine cover story telling the athlete at home that they could "make it" playing professional lacrosse. And that was enough to get picked up by every major media outlet: from ESPN, *Entrepreneur*, Inc. magazine, Fast Company, Yahoo Sports, *The New York Times*, *The Washington Post*, CNBC, and more.

Nolan Ryan was the first million-dollar man in baseball. When his income statement hit the press, more young athletes across America decided to play baseball. Today, MLB players are among the highest paid in the world, with stars making upwards of fifty million per year.

Stories shape perceptions and attract interest. You have an ability to create a captivating narrative around your journey—one that lives in posterity—shaped from history.

I believe that one day, lacrosse players will be making tens of millions of dollars playing the game they love.

THE DIFFERENCE BETWEEN SELF-PROMOTION AND PASSION

I'm not going to convince you to like what I do.
I'm going to show you how much I love what I do.

SELF-WORTH

While today we regard F. Scott Fitzgerald as one of the greatest novelists of the twentieth century, Fitzgerald himself died thinking he was a failure because most of his novels at the time were commercial and critical failures.

"He pinned so much personal hope and ambition and desire and sense of his self-worth as an artist on Gatsby," Fitzgerald's biographer Sarah Churchwell said. "And its comparative failure devastated him."

MVPs, All-Americans, All-Star nominations—all voted on by other people. Popularity, how famous you are. It's all subjective. That's someone telling you what they think your worth is.

The history of sport is filled with people who deserved better. Think of all the talented athletes who never got a shot. Think of Muhammad Ali and Colin Kaepernick—how many years that were lost. Think of the female athletes who should have become household names. I can name you hundreds of lacrosse players who could have had illustrious pro careers if they'd been able to make a living wage playing the game they loved.

Sport is also full of talented people who wanted more than what they got. More money. More recognition. More time.

What some of these folks went through and continue to go through is profoundly unfair. Yet on an individual level, life is unfair. It's unpredictable. People get snubbed, screwed over, misunderstood for many reasons—most of which have nothing to do with social justice.

Which is why all of us have to cultivate a strong sense of self-worth that transcends our moment in time—the trends of the day. Ultimately a champion has to tie their self-worth to their own actions. Because it's the only thing we can control.

I understand that winning MVPs, All-American awards, and other accolades is very satisfying and rewarding. Same goes for making money. Yet I've learned not to let myself be distracted by things that are not really up to me. Instead, I fall in love with the work that will prepare me to win. I strive to play harder than any other person on the field. And to be as good of a human being as I can.

Legendary martial artist and actor Bruce Lee reminds us, "Don't speak negatively about yourself. Even as a joke. Your body doesn't know the difference."

Remember, the greatest champions in history faced adversity, setbacks, and defeats, but they never let those moments define their worth. Instead, they used those experiences to fuel their determination and resilience. Embrace failure as a teacher and you will find that it can be one of the most powerful catalysts for enhancing your self-worth.

had an enormous dream. I wanted to build the next major professional sports league.

But it started with a tiny step. It started with a social media page. I created my first Facebook page in 2008, and posted every day—writing stuff like, "I'm at the gym with my strength and conditioning coach, and here's what we did." [insert pic] "This is my favorite postgame meal!" [insert pic] "Here's my favorite practice drill." [insert video]

Within weeks my audience was growing, and I had an important realization. It's a better business strategy to build a relationship with people first. Trust comes before risk. Authenticity and passion drive interest and engagement.

My first agent told me that the peak of my professional career was already in the rearview mirror. He said, "The most recognizable and most commercial you will ever be is when you played in the National Championship Game in front of 50K people at Gillette Stadium on ESPN." His plan was for us to make as much money as we could in the next three-year period before "the next Paul Rabil plays at Gillette." I'll never forget it. We parted ways a week later.

Within several months I had fifty thousand followers on my Facebook page. The same number of people who were at Gillette Stadium earlier in May.

Then I launched a camp and clinic business.

There was a flywheel effect—my on-field play led to media coverage, which led to social media growth, which led to camp and clinic revenue. Sponsors started to take notice, and within the year I landed my first endorsement.

That call came from Under Armour. It was great for me, as well as the overall visibility of the sport. I remember that for our first marketing campaign, they put me in a ColdGear ad with Dick's Sporting Goods—a commercial that ran on Thanksgiving Day during the NFL games that register fifty million viewers. They're among the most-watched shows on TV every year. Cold-weather gear is functional across every sport, and I happened to be using a lacrosse stick in the ad. They called me, "Paul Rabil, professional lacrosse player." My social media audience grew to over a hundred thousand followers.

Campaigns with Red Bull, GoPro, and Chevrolet followed. *Bloomberg* billed me lacrosse's first million-dollar man. I remember feeling like I had "made it." Playing professional lacrosse had paid off.

Yet, at the same time, I was one of the only ones doing it in pro lacrosse.

Every sport has multiple stars. Some leagues have dozens. Even boxing pits a baby face against a heel. Good versus evil. Favorite versus underdog. Nobody goes at it alone. Nobody wins by themselves. Even Apple has Microsoft, Fox has NBC, McDonald's has Burger King, and Uber has Lyft. Not only did I want my peers in lacrosse to share in my success and opportunity, but I knew it would be good for business.

That was a big reason why my brother, Mike, and I created the Premier Lacrosse League. We launched it arm in arm with 140 of the best players in the world—who received higher wages, health insurance, equity in the league, and a network partner that afforded them the distribution support they so desperately deserved—so their visibility would continue beyond the college National Championship game.

The truth is, when I started that Facebook page, when I left my job in real estate, when I won my first MLL championship, and when I landed my first endorsement, I hadn't yet conceived of the PLL.

And therein lies one of the profound lessons in life. Most things of magnitude start small.

Talking about what he learned from working with Nobel Prize winners, interviewing the great minds of his time, and studying the greatest ever— the mathematician Richard Hamming said that to do great work, you have to "plant little acorns from which the mighty oak trees grow."

Start your first business. Meet your audience where they are. Press *publish* on the first post. Don't wait for all the stars to align.

Take your first shot.

Plant your little acorn.

MIXING FAMILY AND BUSINESS

My business partner is my older brother, Mike.

As far back as I can remember, we competed against each other. We were so competitive that our games often ended in fights. When we were younger, we would play knee football on the carpet in the basement. Every snap was a full-on tackle. One of them ended up with Mike throwing me into a portable heater—and I needed a few stitches on the top of my head. When we got a bit older, we were playing basketball outside, and I had about enough of him fouling me in the post . . . so I turned around and punched him square in the nose.

Very soon after, we had to make a rule that if we were both playing, we had to be on the same team.

Cut to our thirties, still competitive as hell—we kept the rules, building the PLL on the same team.

People often warn against mixing family and business for two reasons. The first is, as cofounders, we have a fiduciary duty to serve our investors and customers first. Well, family comes first, shouldn't it? This can make for difficult decisions if we're not on the same page. The second is more complex. Often in life we treat the people we care about the most with the least amount of respect, and those whom we have just met with the most. My therapist, Dr. Lindsey Hoskins, once told me that when we hurt someone we love, it's because we fear disconnection from that someone. We hope that by lashing out, they'll show us love, and as a result, we'll feel safer in the relationship. That resonated with me.

When I've contemplated the value proposition of working with my brother, the rationales are endless. We have uncompromising loyalty and love for each other. When things don't go our way, we know we have each other to fall back on. When the nights turned to morning, we had the shared resilience and determination to keep going. We're intellectual equals, with skill sets that are compounding in a complex industry. We even saved company funds by sharing a bed in the early days of building. We're on the same team.

I've found that family members most need to mix into their business partnership one thing: honesty. It's critical to talk about your history, your needs, and how you want to grow in the relationship.

For Mike and me, it's a continued work in progress.

In the end, there's no greater joy than working on a dream with someone you love.

OUTWORK YOUR OPPONENT

When Creative Artists Agency (CAA) was just a talent representation firm, Michael Ovitz found himself in a shotgun pitch for Coca-Cola's $300 million a year marketing business against the formidable McCann Erickson—the world's largest advertising company. It was the account's incumbent of forty years, with two hundred people dedicated to servicing the client. Ovitz had just met a few Coke executives at a conference in New York City before coming up with an idea for its on-air commercial strategy. They liked his idea so much that they invited him down to headquarters to properly pitch it.

Here was the issue: Ovitz and CAA weren't in the ad business. How could they compete with best-in-class McCann Erickson?

CAA's founder put together a team of his six most creative people. But that's not where the deal was won.

Coca-Cola scheduled this shotgun pitch for a Tuesday morning at 11:00 in one of its conference rooms just outside of Atlanta. Both companies were invited to present their newest and best concepts that would either win or retain the $300 million account.

Ovitz flew his team in the night before, asked for access to the space so they could familiarize themselves with the technology, then rehearse. Afterward, he took his execs to a nice dinner and bought them Armani suits so they would "look and feel the part."

They arrived the next morning at 10:00 to set up their presentation. In contrast, the McCann team arranged their travel from New York City that morning and scurried in with the same look we all know so well directly off a flight. They hadn't prepared the way CAA did.

Mike and I had never built a pro sports league, much less run a team. We had to viciously study, prepare, and rehearse before every investor call, every sponsorship meeting, and every network pitch. We knew that the twenty-year incumbent, Major League Lacrosse, was taking meetings with the same folks. They were our competition. They had been around much longer than us. They had a full staff. And we had to outwork them.

CAA won Coca-Cola's business that day.

Twenty-five years later, Mike and I found ourselves on Lexington Avenue pitching the world's largest talent, film finance, brand consulting, and sports agency on investing in the PLL.

CAA said yes.

DON'T BECOME A MONSTER

The novelist Jenny Offill opened an essay with a confession:

> My plan was to never get married. I was going to be an art monster
> instead.

An art monster is someone whose work utterly consumes their entire
life. Someone who gives everything to be great at what they do. Someone
like the writer Philip Roth, so utterly trapped in his creative bubble that he
couldn't see how sad it was to proudly say:

> I live alone, there's no one else to be responsible for or to, or to spend
> time with. . . . If I get up at five and I can't sleep and I want to work,
> I go out and I go to work. So I work, I'm on call. I'm like a doctor and
> it's an emergency room. *And I'm the emergency.*

Philip Roth wasn't just driven. He was an unabashed art monster. People
used phrases like "insistently selfish" to describe him. They wrote that, like
the male characters in his books, he treated the females in his life as nothing more than objects. His marriages fell apart. Even his biographer got
Me-Too'd.

Some of the greats of all time were art monsters. Some of the people in
this book *can be* art monsters in their own way. Some were worse than others, but the insanity that made them great was often weaponized against
other people—the heightened focus, the assassin's creed, the pursuit of their
goals while neglecting everything else.

They won a lot, sure . . . but was it always worth it? A journalist once
asked Roth if he ever smiled. "Yes," he said, "when I'm hiding in a corner
and no one sees it."

That's so sad . . .

Is it "success"?

Don't be a monster. Don't be one of the athletes who leave behind a handful of bitter relationships, a rap sheet, used-up people, broken marriages, kids they never saw, shameful secrets they kept.

Don't let your legacy carry the footnote that you were a monster.

TIME TO EVOLVE

Ted Williams's mother was a work monster. She was so consumed with her work at The Salvation Army that she never saw her son—one of the all-time greatest baseball players—play baseball. And his dad—well, Ted was given the middle name Samuel, after his dad, Samuel Williams, and to give you an idea of their relationship, as soon as he was old enough, Ted legally removed his middle name from his birth certificate.

Ted became a sport monster. For much of his career, he was ruthlessly selfish. He cared about nothing other than becoming a better and better baseball player. It paid off. He had a legendary career. He finished with a career batting average of .344, hitting 521 home runs and accumulating 2,654 hits. Ted also had an exceptional ability to get on base—his career on-base percentage of .482 is the highest in MLB history. He was an All-Star nineteen times and won the American League MVP award twice. For his on-field prowess, Ted earned the equivalent of about $19 million.

The downside of all this was that when he had kids, initially, as his parents had done to him, he neglected them.

But this story doesn't have the same sad ending. He evolved out of being a monster—at least as much as he could, with the time he had left.

"What's incredible as an observer," a friend said of a much older Ted Williams, "was to watch him fall in love with his kids. The vulnerability of having love for your children. You could see it just gnaw. It was everything against his grain to succumb to this outside influence of children. Love had control over him. He felt vulnerable. A vulnerability he had never had in his life."

In his diary, his kids slowly began to make more and more appearances. "Claudia, John Henry took canoe ride to Gray Rapids," he wrote in one entry. Then, in another, he praised his son: "His casting is better than I expected so he must have been practicing some. After an aching rest and a few blisters on his casting hand, he is getting a little uninterested. Finally he got his first fish. A grilse. Enthusiasm revived. 3 grilse. Caught his first salmon. 10 pounds. Big day in a young fisherman's life."

What the greats have in common is that they are always trying to get better. In this stage, getting better is less about our craft. It's about becoming balanced in areas where we were once completely imbalanced. It's about evolving out of being completely insane about your craft and into being a well-rounded human being.

THE POWER OF LETTING GO

Letting go is one of the most profound and challenging parts of life.

In the pursuit of greatness, we often find ourselves entangled in a web of attachments and expectations. We cling to our desires, our fears, our past victories, our relationships—believing that they define us.

But there comes a moment in every champion's journey when they must confront a fundamental truth: true power lies in letting go.

Letting go is not a sign of weakness; it's an act of courage and wisdom. It's about releasing burdens that hold us back, so we can free ourselves to take on something better. It's a way to access our full potential.

In 2014, I received a call from my Boston Cannons general manager, Kevin Barney, telling me that I had been traded to the New York Lizards. As he hung up the phone, the weight of his decision settled in. I was gutted. I couldn't believe that the organization that I poured my life into had decided to move in a different direction. I could feel myself gripping to the embarrassment, to the fear, to the unknown. But deep down, I knew that this would become the next part of my journey—the more I held on to Boston, the less I could give to New York.

In the grand theater of our lives, relationships play a starring role. They can be exhilarating, fulfilling, and life-affirming. But sometimes, despite our best intentions and efforts, they can take on another role. In 2017, I went through a divorce—it was the hardest thing I've had to endure in my life.

Letting go of a relationship is not a sign of failure, but a demonstration of courage and self-respect. By releasing what no longer serves us, we can create space for new relationships and opportunities to enter our lives. Along the way, I learned that seeking therapy was helpful in navigating my emotions and processing my feelings—like a great coach will do for their players after a game. I practiced self-care by engaging in activities that brought me newfound joy. And I forgave myself and released the negative emotions that were holding me back.

Divorce was a part of my journey that tested my mettle. It became transformative and strengthening.

In 2021, I retired from playing the game I loved. For athletes, the fear of retiring is connected to a loss of identity. We have spent decades defining ourselves by accomplishments and championships, such that when the pursuit comes to an end, we ask ourselves, "Who am I without my sport?" or "What is my purpose now?"

Ultimately, retirement is a natural part of the journey. It can become a testament to the passion and dedication that fueled our success. I chose to confront the unknown by doing two things: acknowledging the fear of leaving the game behind, and actively preparing for the moment when it would arrive. Doing both helped me retire with confidence and purpose.

Letting go is not a onetime event, but an ongoing practice.

Remember, the power of letting go is not about giving up. It's about taking control of your own destiny. It's about realizing that a true champion is not the one who holds on the tightest, but the one who knows when to release and soar to all new heights.

FIND A COACH

You might think that at this point in your career you don't need any more coaches. That you can figure it all out on your own. That you know your strengths and weaknesses.

In 2002, Google board member John Doerr told Google's new CEO Eric Schmidt that he should hire the football-coach-turned-business-executive Bill Campbell.

"I don't need a coach," Schmidt said. "I'm an established CEO. Why would I need a coach? Is something wrong?"

No, no, no, Doerr assured him. It was nothing personal. "Everybody needs a coach," Doerr said. This is not a controversial idea to an athlete, but in the corporate world, coaches—whether a mentor or a therapist—are rarer, sometimes even frowned upon.

For many reasons, Schmidt was reluctant. He had trouble seeing what he—a proven CEO with a PhD in computer science—could learn from a former football coach about running a technology company. It turned out he had a lot to learn. So much, in fact, that after nearly two decades of working together, Schmidt coauthored a book with Campbell.

In it, Schmidt says hiring a coach was the best thing he ever did. Indeed, Campbell would become known as the trillion-dollar coach for the enormous market cap of the companies and CEOs he worked for.

What coaches offer, especially as we progress in our careers, is a unique perspective and insight that we can't always provide for ourselves. They see our blind spots, challenge our assumptions, and guide us in navigating complexities we might overlook. They bring wisdom that extends beyond our own experiences, ultimately helping us to reach new heights of success.

YOUR JOB IS TO MAKE FAST TRANSITIONS

I used to ask my therapist—a kind of coach who helps me to be a better person—how it's possible that she could have seven or eight really intense sessions in a day.

Dr. Lindsey Hoskins does the following exercise.

She visualizes a bookshelf and imagines that each of her clients is a book on that shelf. Before I walk into her office, she pulls my book out and reviews last week's chapter. Then, she and I together create the next chapter in my book. After I leave her office, she takes a moment to reflect, close the book, then put it back on her bookshelf, where it stays—closed, out of mind—until she sees me again. And then she pulls her next client's book off her bookshelf.

The leadership coach Randall Stutman captures this idea perfectly:

> Your job as a leader is to make really fast transitions. You play many different roles in many different places—your job is to not carry the last conversation to this conversation.

You turn the ball over. One of your colleagues makes a mistake. You get bad news from the product team just before you have to lead a meeting with the marketing team. You get a disgruntled email from a customer just before you walk in the door and have to be Dad.

Your job is to make fast transitions.

The high-performance psychologist Dr. Michael Gervais told me that, early in his career, between clients, he would wash his hands. And he said that while he washed his hands, "I would take a moment and remind myself that I was fully present, I was there for them, and that is *their stuff*." The point was to not carry the last conversation to the next conversation.

Whether you visualize a bookshelf or wash your hands—you need to figure out a practice that works for you. It's a practice similar to a free throw routine—meant to help you transition from the hard foul you just absorbed, or the game-pending pressure you feel before your next shot.

On the field or in the boardroom, whether you're a CEO or a therapist, a captain or a rookie . . . your job is to make really fast transitions.

WHATEVER YOU DO . . .

After winning two national championships and national player of the year awards in college, then four titles, MVP, and Rookie of the Year in the WNBA—Maya Moore stepped away from the game of basketball.

When she signed autographs, Moore signed with a Bible verse, Colossians 3:23: "Whatever you do, work at it with all your heart . . ."

"I've worked my tail off no doubt to get to where I'm at," Moore said when she announced her unexpected departure, "but I also know I've been given an opportunity that's bigger than basketball."

Moore shifted her focus to something beyond the game. In college, she had heard about a man, Jonathan Irons, who at the age of sixteen was wrongfully convicted and sentenced to fifty years in prison. As Moore learned additional information, she decided to use "the platform and the voice that I have" to bring awareness to Irons's case.

A little over a year after she stepped away from the WNBA, at the height of her career, Moore's advocacy helped obtain Irons's release from prison after *twenty-three* years behind bars for something he didn't do.

"When I stepped away," Moore said, "I just really wanted to shift my priorities, to show up for things that I felt were mattering more than being a professional athlete."

When I talk about going beyond the game, I'm not just talking about making a living doing other things. I'm talking about taking the opportunity that's bigger than you and your sport. Using the skills, the influence, the platform you've been given to serve your larger communities. To make your voice heard. To show up for things that matter more than being an athlete.

And whatever you do, give it everything you have.

INSPECT WHAT YOU EXPECT

Two brothers, Ernest and Julio, traveled the country selling grapes from their family vineyard. They became wine-making experts, then started a family business, E. & J. Gallo Winery, in 1933. More than ninety years later, it's still a family-owned business, generating more than $2 billion annually.

I asked the company's CMO Stephanie Gallo what one thing contributes to the company's long-lasting culture during a time of such tremendous growth. She told me that her family's motto is "inspect what you expect."

The best players in the world never ask a teammate to do something they haven't already done themselves. They can demand the effort that they demonstrate. The best coaches in the world don't just study their opponent's film. They obsessively study their own team's practice film—reviewing their players' performance during each drill.

Inspect what you expect.

Lorne Michaels, creator of the late-night sketch comedy phenomenon *Saturday Night Live*, has received twenty-one Primetime Emmy Awards from ninety-eight nominations—a record for the most-nominated individual in the award show's history. Lorne's been a writer on the show, has appeared in numerous sketches over the years, and remains its executive producer. Every show goes off on his watch, with sketches added and subtracted live, and everything ending when he alone decides—sometimes early, sometimes a bit late. It's his show, with his inspection, and his touch.

In both the success story of E. & J. Gallo Winery and the creative realm of *Saturday Night Live*, one common thread emerges—no leader is above the work. The Gallo brothers started their business from the ground up, getting their hands dirty and understanding the intricacies of wine making firsthand. Similarly, the best players and leaders in the world set high standards for their teammates, knowing that they have already walked the path of hard work and dedication themselves.

Lorne Michaels's hands-on approach to *Saturday Night Live* showcases the essence of his expectations—he not only is the mastermind behind the show but actively engages in its creative process, making real-time decisions and molding the show's direction. This commitment to excellence and leading from the front has undoubtedly played a significant role in the show's continued success and cultural impact.

In every domain, whether it's family business, sports, or entertainment, true leadership stems from setting clear expectations and demonstrating the dedication and passion needed to surpass them. When leaders inspect what they expect, they cultivate a lasting culture of excellence that endures.

A CHEMIST, NOT AN INVENTOR

During a snowstorm in 1891, a gym teacher named James Naismith was looking for materials to create an indoor game for his students. He found a soccer ball and two peach baskets. He nailed the baskets at each end of the gym and told his students the idea was to throw the ball through the basket.

Basketball was born.

"The way that human creativity works is recombination," fantasy writer Brandon Sanderson said.

Creativity is the blending together of elements that previously existed separately. You combine a peach basket with a soccer ball and create basketball.

I'm more of a chemist than an inventor. With the PLL, we designed our product based on the best parts of the Big Four sports leagues, the UFC, the MLS, and the X Games.

"We remix," Sanderson said. "We don't come up with a new creature. We put a horn on a horse and call it a unicorn. That's how we create on a fundamental level."

We are chemists, not inventors.

WHO ARE YOUR SEAT BELTS?

Udonis Haslem played twenty seasons in the NBA, all with the Miami Heat. He didn't log a ton of minutes. In the last seven years of his career, he played in just sixty-five total games.

From the outside looking in, Haslem made a lot of money—in his final season alone, he made $2.9 million—even if he didn't play much.

But to those on the inside, Haslem is irreplaceable. The former NBA player Channing Frye talked about how, just like Ferraris have seat belts, every great team has veterans like Haslem. "Udonis Haslem is the seat belt—if anything goes wrong, he locks them up," Frye said. "He is the guy when [stars like] Jimmy Butler or Victor Oladipo want to act crazy, he brings them back into the seat so they're connected and they don't fly off the rails."

Have you ever been on a team stacked with talent but didn't win? I have.

It happens all the time. Because a seat belt like Haslem is rarer than talent.

We've said that we want to treat our bodies like high-performance sports cars. We want to fill our tanks with premium fuel. We want to surround ourselves with other high-performing vehicles. The same is true on the organizational level. Once we have that support, we need to buckle up to get the most out of our drivers.

In the world of sports and in the journey of life, the path to success is often paved with the guidance and support of experienced and stabilizing figures—the "seat belts" that keep us grounded and moving forward. These invaluable mentors and role models can be the driving force behind personal growth, achievement, and lasting impact.

But how do we identify and effectively use these seat belts?

At the heart of this quest lies the art of recognizing the value of experience and wisdom. Whether on the sports field or in life, we must seek out individuals who have walked the path before us and achieved success in their own right. These mentors and role models offer a wealth of insights, guiding us away from pitfalls and toward better decision-making. They are the seasoned veterans who have weathered storms and triumphed, and now they stand ready to offer their guidance to those who seek it.

DRESS THE PART

Jay-Z doesn't wear a suit to business meetings.

He often steps out of the office in a white T-shirt, black jeans, and sneakers, with a green sweatshirt draped over his shoulders and a hat and sunglasses on.

"The clothes are an extension of me," he explains. "I have to stay true to whatever I'm feeling, whatever direction I'm heading in."

When we hosted early investor meetings, I dressed like an athlete, and my brother, Mike, wore a suit. This set the tone of who we were and what we were building. A new professional lacrosse league built by the players, for the players.

Mike was the serial entrepreneur with a résumé to back him up. I was the professional athlete with a background in media. If I came to the meeting in a suit, they would've seen two bankers with no differentiation, and if Mike wore a white T-shirt and black jeans, they may have thought we weren't the right stewards of their capital.

We dressed like ourselves. It was authentic to who we were and dynamic enough for prospective investors to believe we were crazy enough to do it.

The music executive Chris Lighty—who represented artists such as 50 Cent, Busta Rhymes, A Tribe Called Quest, Missy Elliott, LL Cool J, and Mariah Carey—liked to say, "If you want to rob a bank, dress like a banker."

Set the tone for what you're trying to do, who you're trying to be, where you're trying to go.

KEEP WORKING TO GET BETTER

When I was playing in the MLL, we weren't getting much distribution on TV, so the only way to connect with lacrosse fans was through social media. I committed to being an early adopter, learning as much as I could. Every year over the course of the next ten, I would take a trip to Silicon Valley to meet with the sports partnership teams at the various tech platforms—the YouTubes, Instagrams, and Twitters of the world.

I would ask for advice on how to be better on each platform, how to use some of the new tools and gadgets, and so on. Through these visits and my own research, year after year after year, I became an expert in what is now being called "new media."

If given the choice early in my career, I would have chosen to just be an athlete full time. But I can now see that learning social media, learning to understand consumer habits and how to build out creative and thoughtful content all helped me co-found and build the PLL.

The billionaire entrepreneur, investor, and software engineer Marc Andreessen put it bluntly: "I think skill acquisition, literally the acquisition of skills and how to do things, is just dramatically underrated."

Underrated is an understatement.

When I spoke to Mark Cuban—minority owner of the Dallas Mavericks and a "shark" on *Shark Tank*—he said he looks for one thing in players he considers adding to the Mavericks' roster, likewise with entrepreneurs he considers investing in: "Are they working to get better?"

Because in sports, business, and life, things change rapidly. The world is progressing faster than it ever has. It's more competitive than it's ever been. The skills that made you successful a few years ago are not the skills that will make you successful today or tomorrow—the world has moved on. If you are not moving forward, you will be left behind.

TURN YOUR FAILURES INTO YOUR ACCOMPLISHMENTS

Q uentin Tarantino's list of accomplishments has its own Wikipedia page. But the one he's the proudest of isn't listed there.

It's not the many Academy Awards, Golden Globes, or Grammy nominations.

"Of all the accomplishments, the one I'm the most proud of," Tarantino said, "is the two weeks after [his first movie] *My Best Friend's Birthday* failed."

In 1981, when he was seventeen, Tarantino dropped out of school and moved to Hollywood, getting a job at a movie store, Video Archives.

With his Video Archives coworkers, Tarantino began working on his first movie, *My Best Friend's Birthday*. Tarantino worked on the movie for three years. Every dollar he made at Video Archives went into making it.

"I was under the impression that we were making this really amazing thing," he said. He thought it was going to launch his filmmaking career. Tarantino finished *My Best Friend's Birthday* in 1987, and as he showed it to people, "I realized I did not have what I thought I had."

One producer, for instance, said after watching, "Quentin, what you need to do with this tape is, you need to wrap it in the bloodiest steak you can find, and you need to get a little boat, and you need to go out into the ocean and find the sharkiest waters you can find, and then drop this meat-covered tape into the ocean!"

It was "a horrible, embarrassing failure," Tarantino said. "I worked for three years on this movie. It was my dream project . . . And it ended up being nothing. Absolutely nothing! . . . I was very depressed."

And "the fact that I didn't quit," he said, "is the number one thing in life I'm most proud of. Everyone I knew would have quit . . . The fact that I had such a failure and that I didn't give up is the number one thing in my life that I'm the most proud of."

Instead of giving up on his dream of being a filmmaker, Tarantino realized he could reframe the failure. The philosopher Epictetus said, "Every event has two handles," meaning there are always at least two ways to look at every situation.

After a few weeks of being depressed, Tarantino said, "I started looking at it more practically."

He watched the final scene he filmed and compared it to some of the earlier scenes he'd filmed. There was a distinct difference in the quality.

Well, he thought, *that kind of progress is probably why students go to film school.* So, Tarantino said, "Well, that's my film school. I learned how not to make a movie."

Remember what we've said: there are no losses, only lessons. Every loss—whether in sport, personally, monetarily, and so on—can be reframed as a learning opportunity.

DON'T GIVE A SHIT ABOUT SHIT YOU DON'T GIVE A SHIT ABOUT

In 2015, Jeni Britton Bauer got the call you never want to get if you're in her industry. A pint of her Jeni's Splendid Ice Creams tested positive for *Listeria*. Two hundred sixty-five *tons* of ice cream had to be destroyed, costing her company $2.5 million.

"There's stress," Jeni said, "and then there's crisis."

This was a crisis.

Jeni's name was on pints of ice cream in grocery stores and homes nationwide. She had over twenty scoop shops and close to a thousand employees. She'd been doing this for thirteen years. Her response to this crisis could go only one of two ways, she said. "We're either going to save 1,000 jobs and the incredible community we've built or we're going down in flames."

She made the decision to recall and destroy 265 tons of ice cream. Incoming revenue stopped for three weeks as they first worked to determine the source of *Listeria* and then reworked their facilities to make sure they'd avoid any other crises.

Like all the greats, Jeni didn't just navigate the crisis, she brought her company out the other side stronger, better.

"I learned through that process," she said, "what I now say in my head over and over: *I don't give a shit about shit I don't give a shit about.*"

She didn't give a shit about external opinions or judgments from people who weren't directly involved in helping her overcome the crisis. She didn't give a shit about assigning blame for who caused the crisis. She didn't give a shit about anything other than what could contribute to the solution.

When you're trying to recover from a setback or overcome adversity or get out of some funk, do what Jeni did:

Focus on what you care about, what you can affect, and let everything else go.

It takes practice. That's why Jeni says it over and over, like a mantra:

I don't give a shit about shit I don't give a shit about.

The double benefit is that when you let go of all the shit you don't give a shit about, you can give all of you—all of your time and energy—to the shit you *do* give a shit about.

MAKE A'S IN FEWER THINGS

In 2008, Matthew McConaughey got a call from his film production office. He reached to pick up the phone, but his hand paused mid-reach when he saw the caller ID. He didn't want to answer it. He let the call go to voicemail, then he called his lawyer.

"I'm shutting down the production company immediately," he said. "Shut down J.K. Livin Records as well."

It was too much.

"I had five things on my proverbial desk to tend to daily: family, foundation, acting, a production company, and a music label," McConaughey writes. "I felt like I was making B's in all five. I was majoring in my minors. By shutting down the production company and the music label, I got rid of two minors with plans to major in my majors, to make A's in three things."

He said it like it was easy, but this must have been hard. So hard. Unpleasant conversations. Tears. Expensive severances—which he insisted on. People who tried to convince him to stick with it. Embarrassment at having made promises and commitments he couldn't keep.

So he carefully shut down the businesses to take care of the stuff on his desk that was most important. He would focus entirely on his family, his foundation, and his acting career. He was insane about his craft, his family, and his foundation.

You might try to rationalize ways in which you're the exception, but you're not. You can't do it all. I couldn't. I haven't come across anyone able to make A's in more than a select few things. It was this realization that led to my decision to retire when I did. I was making B's in too many things. I wanted to focus exclusively on the PLL, producing great stories, and my personal life.

"Simplify, focus, conserve to liberate," McConaughey writes.

All right, all right, all right.

LEAVING ON A HIGH NOTE

Just before the ninth season of *Seinfeld* in 1998, Jerry Seinfeld was offered $110 million to do one more season of the show. He turned down the money and walked away from the show when it was at the height of its popularity.

Seinfeld likes to say that being a stand-up comedian is like being a surfer—it's just you and your board. Running a TV series, on the other hand, is like operating a big boat—there's a lot of people and a lot of money required to maintain its progress through the water.

Seinfeld stopped the show, he said, "before it stopped moving through the water in the beautiful way that it was moving."

It wasn't just that he didn't want to be on a boat that was struggling across the water. More than that, he didn't want the audience to have that experience. "The love affair between the people that were making the show and the audience was so intense," he said. "It was so white hot. I had to respect that and I could not let it go to that point where it starts to age and wither." A small amount of too much of anything, Seinfeld said, can totally alter our perception of the thing.

The movie that was good but dragged on a little too long—we just remember that it dragged on. The guest who was cool but stayed a little past their welcome—we just remember that they stayed too long. The athlete who had a great career but should have hung 'em up a little sooner—we just remember that they should have retired earlier.

I took a risk to go all in on lacrosse, I went through a difficult divorce, and at some point I had to make the decision to retire from the game I love the most. From these painful decisions, I can tell you what you already know: it's really hard to know when to end it, when to quit, when to call it a night, when to walk away, when to retire. It's an art, not a science.

In that ninth and final season of *Seinfeld*, there's an episode all about "getting out on a high note." Of course, it's not always something we get to decide. Your coach can decide to cut you. Your boss can decide to lay you off. Your partner can decide to leave you. But when it is up to you, this is a good rule of thumb. Whether it's a TV series, a career, or a relationship— try to get out on a high note.

OVER-REWARD THE ASSIST

Mike Levine, the head of CAA Sports, is the top dog at the biggest sports agency in the world, and he shares an office. By choice.

When CAA Sports was founded in 2007, Levine worked out of a "surrogate step-child office," as he referred to it on my podcast. It was just an open floor with a couple of old desks for him and his only employee, Paul Danforth. They gained enough traction to build out a team and, eventually, to move into a beautiful building in New York City.

When Levine was shown the floor plan, his and Paul's offices were next to each other. "This looks great," he told his COO. "But can we just not put up that wall between mine and Paul's office?"

"Are you sure?" the COO replied. "There's no executive at CAA who shares an office."

Levine was sure. It wasn't just about setting an example for his employees. It was about something he fundamentally believes—that the success of a company boils down to teamwork.

"We have found that a team sport atmosphere is critical," he said. "So we are an organization that likes to over-reward the assist."

We announced the Premier Lacrosse League on October 22, 2018. Later that week, we unveiled our charitable effort, called PLL Assists. While we knew we could change the professional game, pay our players higher wages, market and distribute the games nationally and internationally—we knew the long-term growth of the game was going to be at the community level.

Lacrosse, like hockey and golf, is an expensive sport to play. You need a helmet, stick, shoulder pads, elbow pads, gloves, and balls. Different from soccer or basketball in America, there's an investment that has to happen before you find out if it's a game that you like to play. Therein lies an opportunity for expensive sports—if we want more people to try lacrosse, we need to reverse the order of investment to "play first."

We make equipment contributions to our PLL Assists partners—from

Harlem Lacrosse to Oakland Lacrosse. We call this our "sticks in hands" initiative.

And when I retired from the game in 2021, I launched a new project called Goals for Greatness, with a mission of putting two goals in all fifty states, every year.

The best way to grow is to give.

This last PLL season indicated that shots taken from a pass have a 10 percent greater likelihood of scoring. Over-reward the assist. Let's put an emphasis on that.

THIS IS TRUE SUCCESS

A coaching tree refers to the lineage of coaches who have been influenced and mentored by a specific head coach. It is the best measure—even better than number of wins or championships—of coaching success: What did those who worked under you go on to do?

Lorne Michaels, the creator of *Saturday Night Live*, has one of the greatest trees of all time. He said his mission is "to find the most talented people of my time."

Mission accomplished.

Lorne has discovered and developed many of the biggest names in show business: Chevy Chase, John Belushi, Bill Murray, Eddie Murphy, Mike Myers, Chris Farley, Will Ferrell, David Spade, Tina Fey, Amy Poehler, Jimmy Fallon, Kate McKinnon, Kenan Thompson, and on and on. Lorne's tree is also responsible for movies such as *Wayne's World*, *Tommy Boy*, and *Mean Girls*, as well as TV shows like *30 Rock* and *The Tonight Show*.

General Electric is known for its world-class performance-review process and the dismissal of employees who perform in the bottom 10 percent. It's a criterion that Jim Collins, author of the bestselling book *Good to Great*, says funnels into the company's greatest attribute—leadership. One in every five CEOs running one of roughly 1,100 publicly traded companies with a market value of at least $2 billion has at some point held a job at one of just twenty companies. Thirty-six of these CEOs worked at GE.

Along with winning three Super Bowls, Bill Walsh nurtured coaches like Mike Holmgren, Jon Gruden, Andy Reid, and George Seifert—all of whom went on to achieve great success as head coaches in the NFL.

Five-time NBA champion Gregg Popovich's coaching tree is more like a coaching forest. Current or former NBA head coaches Mike Brown, Mike Budenholzer, Monty Williams, Becky Hammon, Steve Kerr, Ime Udoka, Doc Rivers, Sam Presti, and Taylor Jenkins all played for or coached under Pop.

This is the true measure of success: How many other successful careers trace their roots back to you?

APPEAR TO BE AN OBJECT OF DESIRE

Over a century ago, when baseball first started, ticket sales drove the most revenue. Nowadays, ticket sales revenue falls short of media rights value, sponsorship sales, merchandise, and youth revenue.

Great, I thought, *we can execute against a business plan in that order. We'll be fine.*

Wrong. Quickly, we realized that when it comes to the psychology of a sports fan, success is based on the number of butts in seats—or worse, how many empty seats are left in the stands.

If there's light attendance, the broadcast team will try to shoot as close to field level as possible. By comparison, if you sell out a stadium, the network will spend most of the game panning the crowd, showing every supporter in the stands screaming for their team. Think about it: If you're driving past a restaurant with a line wrapped around the street, you're intrigued. *It must be good.* And if you walk into an empty restaurant, you'll likely turn around.

The French thinker René Girard, famous for his theory of mimetic desire, said, "[A person] will desire any object so long as he is convinced that it is desired by another person."

This is why we launched the PLL under a touring model. Lacrosse didn't have the audience size to support a city-based model . . . yet. We wanted to build scarcity—supply and demand. And we wanted to make sure that when we played in a city, every team, player, sponsor, and executive was there. It had to become the best show in town.

Like Lorne Michaels, Mike and I walk the field on game days.

Selling a ticket is one of the hardest things to do in our business. It requires hand-to-hand combat, flexibility, and care. We no longer look at the revenue every ticket brings to the company on a one-to-one basis of revenue in other categories. Selling a ticket is a relationship based on quality and trust. Selling a ticket leads to an increase in media rights, sponsorship, merchandise, and youth participation.

LISTEN

Early in his career, a mentor gave Mark Cuban some feedback, which he still uses today.

He loved Mark's enthusiasm, curiosity, and eagerness, but said he needed to learn to contain it. Especially in meetings. He would talk over people—often because he already knew the answer to the problem. He had done the work in advance.

He told Mark to write the word *LISTEN* at the top of his notepad before every meeting. From then on, before every meeting, every important phone call, every pitch—on *Shark Tank* or otherwise—Mark wrote *LISTEN* at the top of his notepad.

I love the gentle reminder from the Dalai Lama, "When you talk, you are only repeating what you already know. But if you listen, you may learn something new."

You have two ears and one mouth for a reason. You gain so much more from listening to others than from listening to yourself say what you already know.

You never learn anything new while you're talking.

LISTEN.

ASK FOR HELP

Commonly, people building a company, leading an organization, and managing a team, fall into the same trap. They don't ask for help. They feel they can't or shouldn't. That they are supposed to be the one who has all the answers. That they are supposed to be the one doing the helping.

Same thing on the field. If you ask your coach for direction, it might be implied that you didn't study the playbook. Or worse—you *don't care*.

In a study of over twenty thousand people in positions of leadership, researchers found that the top characteristic leaders struggle with is asking for help.

But the greats know that being vulnerable and asking for help are superpowers. Steve Jobs, while he was simultaneously the CEO of Apple Inc. and Pixar Animation Studios, said that building a great business is like "trying to climb a mountain with a whole party of people. [There's] a lot of stuff to bring up the mountain. So one person can't do it alone."

Howard Schultz, who took over as CEO of Starbucks in 1987 when there were only six stores and grew it into a global empire with more than thirty thousand locations around the world, said, "The most undervalued characteristic of leadership is vulnerability and asking for help."

Magic Johnson was one of basketball's greatest players. As a five-time NBA champion and three-time MVP, a major part of his success was his curiosity and inquisitiveness. In the early 1980s, Magic reached out to the Lakers' public relations team to ask for the names and phone numbers of everyone who was sitting courtside at his games. "I cold-called twenty people and said, 'Will you go to lunch with me?'" he recalls. "And they said, 'Yeah.'" Magic wanted to ask what made them successful and if there were ways he could help. Over his thirteen-year career, Magic accumulated almost $40 million dollars in salary. Today, he's a billionaire. Among ownership in the Los Angeles Dodgers, the Washington Commanders, the Los Angeles Sparks, and LAFC, one of Magic's first investments was in . . . Starbucks.

A company whose franchises are all corporately owned, except the 125 locations that Magic negotiated with Howard Schultz over a lunch.

Asking for help was difficult for me. I lacked vulnerability and wanted to prove to my coaches and teammates that I could get the job done myself. But most of the time, I couldn't. So when I finally started practicing asking for help, I discovered three things. First, I rarely found anyone who didn't want to help. People love to help. Second, I found I was building stronger relationships with those whom I showed this type of vulnerability toward. They could trust me. Asking for help is a pillar of honesty. And third, I was able to improve and get things done much faster with help.

Schultz agreed: "Business is built on relationships. Relationships are built on trust. And trust is built on vulnerability and transparency."

So in whatever position of leadership or followership you occupy, ask for help.

Be vulnerable.

In business, sports, and life—vulnerability doesn't make you weak. It makes you an outlier. It's magic.

A DEEP BREATH

I n the second episode of *7 Days Out*, Eleven Madison Park restaurateur Will Guidara catches a mistake made by his electrical contractor. It was apparent that Guidara considered losing his temper on the guy but made a conscious choice not to.

Guidara was later asked what was going through his head in that moment and how he kept his composure.

For context, he first described the "Make It Nice Field Manual"—his restaurant group's internal collection of the principles that guide what they do. One of those principles is "DBC"—Deep Breathing Club. DBC comes from Guidara's longtime friend who, along with setting up and running a recording studio in a psychiatric hospital to try to make therapy cool, became disenchanted with the amount of medication prescribed across the medical world and set out to find better modalities. That led to his discovery of deep breathing's power to heal, soothe, and connect.

"Restaurants," Guidara explains, "are not altogether that much different from a psychiatric hospital." Restaurants, he says, are about relationships, service, and catering to each customer's needs while reacting to what's thrown at you in real time.

So, Guidara says, the worst thing anyone can do in a restaurant is lose their cool. Sometimes, "just taking a deep breath reminds you of what you're trying to accomplish."

In that space provided by the deep breath, Guidara said he was thinking about his ultimate objective. Then he worked backwards to a response that gave him the best chance of getting there. The ultimate objective was definitely not making himself feel better by making someone else feel worse.

The deep breath is one of the most undertaught and underutilized leadership tactics. Look no further than our country's finest protectors—Navy SEALS. They regularly practice box breathing. Four seconds in. Four seconds hold. Four seconds out. Four seconds hold. Repeat.

The simple act of taking a deep breath promotes self-regulation, empathy, and the ability to make thoughtful decisions that benefit the collective goals rather than seeking immediate personal gratification. It creates a space for introspection, can transform how you respond to challenges, and can get the best out of others.

THE WORST BUSINESS TO BE IN

Part of becoming a champion is continuously setting the bar higher and higher for yourself. I was expecting to have a big season in 2020. I worked my ass off in the offseason. I had an awesome training camp. I was ready.

It didn't go as planned.

ESPN analyst Paul Carcaterra said, "This, unequivocally, was the worst I have seen Paul Rabil play . . . was this the end of his reign?" Social media flooded with commentary about whether or not I was cut out for the pro game anymore. They began to question the integrity of the PLL if I continued to play.

I expected the negativity. I knew it was coming. There's a lot of league marketing around me. I post a lot on social media. One could say—I set myself up.

I understood that if I didn't perform, people were going to tear me down. And they did.

Two years after retirement, my perception on that has changed: this was a good thing for lacrosse. It's not what I wanted. But that level of banter is commonplace for major pro sports leagues. Four-time MVP, four-time Finals MVP, four-time NBA champion, two-time Olympic gold medalist, and the NBA's all-time leading scorer, LeBron James, faces criticism for his play every season—almost every game. When you're in the public eye, expect the public to have a word with you.

When you don't play well and fans don't tell you about it, they don't care. And there's no worse business to be in than one that people don't care about.

Every athlete learns this: you'd rather play to boos than to no crowd at all. The same goes for critics, doubters, and bad headlines.

Silence? That smothers you. Criticism? You can use it as fuel.

You know what I did the following season? I led all PLL midfielders in scoring and was voted First-Team All-Pro for the twelfth time in my career. That was my final season.

I couldn't have done it without 'em.

SHOW, DON'T TELL

A couple of friends of mine run an EdTech company. Just before the PLL launched, I pitched them on sponsoring the league. No interest.

In year one, they came to our games at Homewood Field in Baltimore. Homewood Field is one of the most historic lacrosse venues in the world. It was also our first sellout crowd.

After the games, sitting there among the packed house, these two friends came over to me and said, "We want to sponsor the DC games in two weeks."

You can have compelling pitch materials. You can network and work a room with the best of them. You can have a proposal that pencils out better than any of your competitors'. You can have belief, confidence, passion, and all the rest. You can even ask your friends for help.

But if you don't have butts in seats, you've got nothing.

Corporate partners want to see how many people care. Coaches want to see how many points you have. Publishers want to see how many readers you can get. Customers want to see how many bad reviews your product has. And investors want to see how much revenue you can generate.

"Great," Kevin O'Leary likes to say right after a *Shark Tank* pitch. "Now show me the money!"

Don't tell us how good you are. Show us.

WE'LL SEE

There's an old story I love about a Chinese farmer.

The Chinese farmer and his son have one horse, which helps the son operate the hoe needed to turn the soil over. One day, the horse takes off and runs for the hills. The son runs inside and says, "Dad, you're not going to believe it—the horse ran away. This is horrible. We're going to die out here." The father, nonchalant, says, "I don't know if it's horrible or not, son, we'll see."

The son is baffled. A few days later, the son is sitting on the porch when he sees the horse running toward him. Behind the horse, there are fifty wild stallions. The son runs to open the paddock and then close it behind all the horses.

He runs inside and says, "Dad, you're not going to believe—the horse returned. With fifty stallions! This is a miracle. We're going to be rich." The father, nonchalant, says, "I don't know if it's a miracle or not, son, we'll see."

A few more days pass. While the son is trying to harness one of the new stallions to the hoe, the horse panics, kicks, and shatters the son's leg. When the father learns what happened, once again, he's nonchalant: "We'll see."

The next day, hundreds of soldiers on horseback show up and the general gets off his horse to inform them that a war is on the horizon and they've instituted the mandatory conscription of men between the ages of seventeen and thirty-five.

The father, well beyond the age range, points at his son's leg and tells the general that he'd be useless in battle. The general agrees and they ride off. The son can't believe his luck. But the father says, "I don't know if you got lucky or not, son, we'll see."

I've lost championship and gold medal games, gotten traded multiple times, been through a divorce, made bad investments and worse life decisions. I've come out on the other side understanding that there is no "good" or "bad." Life is complicated. In the moment at least, you can't call it. Horrible things lead to incredible things, and vice versa, all the time.

Best to accept all that happens. To embrace all that happens. To say to all that happens . . .

We'll see.

PAVE YOUR PATH

n the early 1990s, six years into his career as co-director of marketing and corporate sponsorships for NFL Properties, Don Garber was fired.

Instead of having co-directors, the executives decided to go with one person in charge of the sponsorships department. One of those execs told Garber, "We made a decision, and you're out."

It was all too sudden for Garber. "What do you mean, I'm out?"

"It's been a good run," his boss said. "But the business just isn't generating enough revenue."

Garber could have been bitter. He could have been pissed off. He could have made a scene.

Instead he said, "Listen, why don't you let me take the weekend. I've been thinking about a whole bunch of things. Let me see if I can find an area that's being underserved, and I'll come back to you with a plan."

"Absolutely," Garber's boss said. "If you can find something that can generate revenue for us, that can fill a void, I'm all ears."

Garber didn't say he had been thinking about a whole bunch of things just to buy himself a little time. He really had been. He had been thinking about ways to improve the management and distribution for the NFL's hard-earned and very valuable intellectual property. He had been thinking about ways to bring the game and the players closer to the fans. And he had been thinking of ways to make the league's most valuable TV games even more valuable.

The potential of being fired forced Garber to turn those ideas into a plan that could be executed against. That weekend, he coalesced his ideas into a new division named NFL Business Development and Special Events. In this plan, Garber included ideas for events like the NFL Experience—a fan-interactive festival at the Super Bowl. He included the idea to relaunch the Punt, Pass, and Kick competition to grow participation among young people. He had the idea to create the NFL Skills Challenge to show "who these players are without their helmets and shoulder pads." He had the idea to sell a performance slot during *Monday Night Football* to record companies and their biggest stars. Since the first Super Bowl in 1967, marching bands and instrumentalists performed at halftime—Garber had the idea to have Michael Jackson headline.

"So I wrote that plan," Garber told me, "and they loved it." They took it and pitched it to the NFL commissioner, Paul Tagliabue. And he loved it.

The NFL Business Development and Special Events division was a huge success. It quickly became responsible for generating more revenue than the sponsorships division. So in 1999, Commissioner Tagliabue asked Garber if he had any ideas to expand the NFL's brand beyond the United States. Garber then became senior vice president and managing director of NFL International. His job was to figure out how to grow the NFL's intellectual property around the world. In that role, he reported to a committee chaired by two NFL owners—Lamar Hunt of the Kansas City Chiefs and Robert Kraft of the New England Patriots—who were also the founders of Major League Soccer.

The MLS was then five years into its existence, and roughly $250 million in the hole. Hunt and Kraft were on the brink of folding the league. Impressed with Garber's ability to figure out creative ways for the NFL to generate revenue, Kraft approached Garber at the 1999 NFL owners meeting. He asked, "What do you know about soccer?"

Garber was honest and said he didn't know much. "We're about to change that," Kraft said. And after conversations with Hunt, then Tagliabue, Garber said, "By the end of the weekend, I had been traded. I went from selling American football overseas to selling the real football here in the United States."

With Garber as commissioner, MLS would secure major media partnerships with ESPN, Fox Sports, Univision, and TSN, as well as corporate partnerships with the biggest brands in the world—Adidas, AT&T, Audi, and Coca-Cola included. Garber changed rules on-field to align the league with how the game is played internationally. He created designated player exemptions that led to the acquisition of global superstars like David Beckham, Zlatan Ibrahimovic, and Lionel Messi.

At the time of this writing, there are twenty-nine franchises in the MLS, up from ten when Garber took over in 1999. Those franchises are worth an estimated $582 million apiece, with Forbes giving the league's highest valuation to LAFC, coming in at a staggering $1 billion.

"The key thing," Garber told me, "after NFL Properties told me I was out, I didn't go home and cry. I just knew that I had more still to do at the NFL. But I also knew that the NFL had a lot of holes. Even a powerful brand like that was not being served in all of the areas of opportunity."

It's remarkable to think about where both the NFL and the MLS would be today if Garber had responded to being fired as most people do. If he had just packed up, gone home, and started looking for a new job.

Instead, Garber took ownership of the situation and created a plan that would shape the trajectory of professional sports. This is the way of the champion. In the face of failure, they create opportunity.

Garber said, "We'll see."

NEVER GIVE UP

In his late thirties, Rich Roll was, in his words, "an overweight, out of shape, workaholic, classic couch potato sliding into middle age."

Despite a life of success and material comfort, "I was depressed, discontent, disillusioned with this all-consuming career that I didn't feel like I even consciously chose for myself, suffocating on the promise of this American dream that I felt in my heart was failing to deliver on its implicit guarantee, which was happiness."

Just after his fortieth birthday, Rich reached a crisis point. Midway up the flight of stairs to his bedroom, he had to pause. Out of breath with tightness in his chest and sweat on his brow, he keeled over. He thought this was it. Heart disease runs in his family. Death was now at his door.

And in that moment, he promised himself: *If I make it to tomorrow, I will stop neglecting my health.*

Rich made it through. He changed his diet. A former Stanford swimmer, he rediscovered his love for swimming. He started running and biking.

With a newfound vitality, Rich set out to test his physical and mental capabilities as an ultra-endurance athlete. He completed several grueling endurance races, including the EPIC5 Challenge, which involved completing five Ironman-distance triathlons on five Hawaiian islands in under a week.

In a viral post in 2018, Roll reminded us that there is always still so much to accomplish:

> I didn't reach my athletic peak until I was 43.
> I didn't write my first book until I was 44.
> I didn't start my podcast until I was 45.
> At 30, I thought my life was over.
> At 52, I know it's just beginning.

Keep running. Never give up. And watch your kite soar.

Whether it's during a career transition, or a midlife crisis, take heart in Rich Roll's words and live by his example.

Where you are on your journey, it's just the beginning.

Keep going, never give up, and watch your own kite soar to new heights.

DANCE EVERY NIGHT

I met a couple who have been happily married for sixty-four years.

Their romance began in high school. Three years later they were married. And when I asked how they stayed happily married for so long, the wife answered, "We danced every night."

A lesson I have taken to heart.

I leave a love letter for my partner every day.

I call my parents at least once a week.

I send a text message to my friends to check in every month.

Before every game, I made three behind-the-back passes to my Johns Hopkins teammate Garrett Stanwick.

Having a ritual will foster a deeper, more spiritual connection with your romantic partner, your family, a friend, coach, or teammate.

Find your dance—and keep dancing.

LEAVE THE WORLD BETTER THAN YOU FOUND IT

I grew up playing lacrosse out of pure love and passion.

I wanted to win championships at every level and play for Team USA in the Olympics.

Lacrosse was once a fully sanctioned Olympic sport. In 1904, two Canadian teams and a U.S. team competed at the games in St. Louis, Missouri. In 1908, a team from Canada and a team from Great Britain competed at the games in London. Canada won both gold medals.

As the Olympics evolved, the criteria required to earn International Olympic Committee (IOC) membership changed. Sport participation needed to include both genders, increased international federation participation was required, parity of play among countries was measured, and new economic considerations were slated, among others.

Lacrosse was dropped from the Olympics.

For the greater part of the last two decades, new leadership has been working to get our game back on the world's stage. In fact, part of our early PLL investor materials included the number of countries now playing lacrosse—we're at ninety and growing.

In 2018, the IOC once again granted lacrosse provisional recognition. And in 2021, after I retired, I was asked to join a five-member committee that pitched Los Angeles 2028 and the IOC on why lacrosse deserves to be back in the Olympic Games.

I believed this would be a game-changing achievement for the sport. The Olympics can become the dream for a generation of young lacrosse players around the world.

The same dream I had.

On October 16, 2023, the IOC officially welcomed lacrosse back into the Olympics.

And while I won't be playing, I'll be watching with pure love and passion.

WE ARE SOON FORGOTTEN

What do Ron Dayne, Danny Wuerffel, Rashaan Salaam, and Gino Torretta have in common?

Not long ago, those names were at the top of the college football world. But how many people still remember the names of every Heisman Trophy winner in the '90s?

How about who led the NBA in points in 2012?

How about 2022?

Can you name four Tewaaraton Award winners?

In a book about an eighty-three-day trip around Scotland, Samuel Johnson wrote about a cemetery of Scottish kings so old that the identities of the people in the large underground vaults had been lost. "The graves are very numerous," he observed, "and some of them undoubtedly contain the remains of men who did not expect to be so soon forgotten."

Even those who once shined brightest fade quickly. Lasting fame is a fallacy. It is a pointless pursuit. We are so soon forgotten.

Remembering this helps me keep perspective on what's actually important—my level of personal fulfillment and the strength of connection with loved ones.

FORGET ME

Abby Wambach won a World Cup, two Olympic gold medals, professional and NCAA championships. Few athletes in any sport have ever matched this medley of feats.

When she retired, Wambach said farewell in the most unique way. Most athletes think about legacy. They want to be remembered. They want to be heralded. They want to be put on a pedestal.

Not Abby.

In a Gatorade tribute commercial, Abby sits in front of her locker in street clothes. A moving instrumental plays as she cleans out her locker. She reaches for her captain's armband, lets out a deep breath, and the voice-over begins:

> Forget me. Forget I've ever existed. Forget the medals won, the records broken and the sacrifices made. I want to leave a legacy where the ball keeps rolling forward. Where the next generation accomplishes things so great, that I'm no longer remembered. So forget me, because the day I'm forgotten is the day we will succeed.

In this lifetime, I've had the distinct honor and privilege to play the Indigenous game of America. I've competed at every level—from amateur to professional to international. The game has been my teacher.

As Mike and I began to build the PLL, we knew that the early days would rely heavily on my relationships with the players of Major League Lacrosse, my existing sponsorship portfolio, and our ability to convince investors and potential network partners that we could build this league from scratch.

For over a decade I have been featured in national ad campaigns and invited on *SportsCenter* to promote the game. I've enjoyed every second of it. But in my heart I know a lagging indicator of success for the PLL will be when I am no longer booked for ad campaigns and *SportsCenter* hits. By then, we'll have built a professional sports league whose players are being cast in global campaigns, with games highlighted on ESPN and player interviews on the *TODAY* show, *Good Morning America*, and late-night television.

Here's the hard truth for any player, coach, teacher, therapist, founder, or parent: your greatest work is done when you are no longer needed.

True mastery is not just about the physical prowess, but about inner strength and clarity of purpose.

Forgetting ourselves is the path to finding our true self. With this newfound determination, we can be equipped with the tools to take on our greatest competitors and the most formidable opponent—*yourself.*

ACKNOWLEDGMENTS

My first debt of gratitude goes to every champion who has graciously taken the time to share their story with me. For those who continue to pursue greatness in the dark, and to the champion who is no longer with us, may you rest in power.

To my partners on this project. First, the wonderfully talented and acclaimed writer, Ryan Holiday. From the moment you called with the idea, to your creative and editorial input—thank you a million times. For his extended research and editing contributions, as well as the occasional trip to a PLL game weekend—a major thank-you goes to the *Daily Stoic*'s Billy Oppenheimer. To my exceptionally gifted and gracious editor, Noah Schwartzberg—much like the coaches I had the privilege of playing for, you put the best game plan in front of my first book. To my publisher, Adrian Zackheim, and the spectacular team at Penguin Group's Portfolio—your belief in our vision and your timeless patience were the secret to finishing what could've been an endless pursuit. And to my literary agents, Anthony, David, and the entire CAA team, thank you for believing in me.

After my first few lacrosse practices, I told my mom that I wanted to quit. She proceeded to teach me a very important and first lesson on commitment. It wasn't easy—I would scoff at her in the car on the way to every practice for a month. Without her, I wouldn't have played this beautiful game.

Beginning with my undergrad campaign at Johns Hopkins, through every pro and international match, my dad would send me an email on game days. He would describe the champion's mindset, forecast the vibe in the venue, leave a few remarks on the opponent, and pray for safety on both sides of the ball. It felt motivating and safe to get these from him. It also instilled the value of writing and documenting within me.

One of my favorite chapters in this book is about planting "little acorns." Had it not been for the biggest acorn in the family, who left his job to build the PLL with me . . . well, I'd just be a retired athlete, continuing the pursuit of my next professional life. Thank you for everything, Mike.

My sister is the toughest person in the family. She moves effortlessly through her successes and challenges, and I only hope that these chapters can be as succinct and creative as she is.

To my extraordinary and loving partner, Vanessa. Your support and enthusiasm around this project were everything—and your prowess for storytelling meaningfully contributed to the life that lives on these pages.

My inward journey began with renowned sports psychologist Dr. John Eliot. I had lost my sense of self and was completely engulfed in my career, a workaholic who needed to get healthy. Together, we worked on my relationship to the game so that I could begin to build a new relationship with myself and others.

To my LMFT and LMHC, Dr. Lindsey Hoskins. I would like to express my deepest gratitude for your dedication to my personal growth. Always leading with endless empathy and intellectual investigation, your guidance and insights have played a pivotal role in shaping my understanding of the topics discussed in this book.

When I began playing lacrosse, I fell in love with the game's artisanship. At thirteen, I taught myself how to string my first stick. As I grew older, I fell in love with the competition—the pursuit of winning. However, it wasn't until the twilight years of my career that I truly studied the history of the game—one that stretches back millennia in North America. I haven't found anything as profoundly connected to the origins of this land as a hickory stick. We're all connected in some way—if you pay close enough attention.

To Colin Rosenblum, Samir Chaudry, Brett Roberts, Liam Murphy, Josh Barrow, Mick Davis, David Acker, and everyone who shared their creative and thought-provoking input with me. Thank you for supporting my speculative endeavors with your brilliant touch of art and design.

When I launched my podcast in 2017, my concerns were that "nobody's gonna listen" and "nobody's gonna say yes to an interview." To every world-class athlete, author, entrepreneur, entertainer, politician, and leader who gracefully indulged my long-winded questions—thank you. Your honesty was instrumental in bringing this book to life.

To every head, assistant, and volunteer coach I've had the pleasure of playing for—thank you for your leadership and competitive fire. To my high school coach, Dick Long, I always admired your attention to detail, yet our annual holiday breakfast in Baltimore was something I looked forward to most—well beyond our time on-field together. To my college coach, Dave Pietramala, you helped instill the competitive ferocity, work ethic, and values that I cherish most. To the late Chris Hall—my professional head coach in Washington—he taught me that no matter the means, the best commitments you can make are to yourself and your teammates. A love-hate letter should go to strength and conditioning coaches everywhere—but especially mine of almost twenty years, Jay Dyer. Every warmup, every sprint, every lift, every shot, every stretch, and every long pep talk were well beyond worth it. It was grueling, and I would do it all over again with you. And, of course, to the coach of all coaches, Bill Belichick. From the moment you took ten minutes to meet with me in 2007 to the very generous foreword you wrote for this book—thank you.

To Jackson Tolmach and today's high school recruits, I know how bad you want it because I was just like you. The difference is that I competed in an era without social media, club lacrosse, early recruiting, and transfer portals. Keep your head down, keep working hard, keep loving the game, and let the other stuff come and go as it pleases.

To my formidable opponents. Those of you who pushed me over the edge—the bitter rivalries and deafening defeats. Without you, I wouldn't have learned some of the most important lessons in sport. The way to the glory of victory is through the dying of defeat.

And to my teammates—from Montgomery Village to DeMatha High School and Johns Hopkins University, in Boston, New York, Washington, Philadelphia, the PLL, and with Team USA. Competing next to you has been the privilege of a lifetime. No job or exhibition will ever feel quite like the intensity and tension of a locker room before a championship game. You've got a brother in me for life.